Unlocking the Clubhouse

Unlocking the Clubhouse

Women in Computing

Jane Margolis and Allan Fisher

The MIT Press
Cambridge, Massachusetts
London, England

This book was set in Sabon by Achorn Graphic Services, Inc.

Printed and bound in the United States of America.

Library of Congress Cataloging-in-Publication Data

Margolis, Jane.
    Unlocking the clubhouse : women in computing / Jane Margolis and Allan Fisher.
        p. cm.
    Includes bibliographical references and index.
    ISBN 0-262-13398-9 (hc. : alk. paper)
    1. Computer science—Vocational guidance. 2. Women in computer science.
I. Fisher, Allan. II. Title.

QA76.25 M35 2001
004′.023—dc21   2001034296

Contents

Acknowledgments

Many people have contributed to the work behind this book. Faye Miller, our research associate, carried out many interviews and much data analysis. Faye's attention to nuance, and her concern that we consider every single voice until we "get it right," played an invaluable role in our research. Jo Sanders co-designed our high school teachers' program and has been a consistent source of good advice; Mark Stehlik played a critical role in building the program; Terri Sawdon made it work. Elaine Seymour has been a constant source of support and insight.

We have benefited from many discussions with our Pittsburgh colleagues, Barbara Lazarus, Janet Schofield, Janet Stocks, and Indira Nair. We are particularly indebted to Barbara for introducing us in the first place and for guiding us to funding. We've learned much from our friends and colleagues Sheila Humphreys, Anita Borg, Paula Rayman, Elizabeth Debold, Pat Campbell, Beryl Minkle, Noah Chevalier, Pattie Heyman, and Kathryn Portnow. Our colleagues in the Carnegie Mellon School of Computer Science—Jim Morris, Jim Roberts, Raj Reddy, Lenore Blum, and Catherine Copetas—have been consistently helpful and supportive. Jane's new colleagues, Helen Astin, Jeannie Oakes, Linda Sax, Yasmin Kafai, and Laurette Cano lent an ear and provided support. Our funders—Ted Greenwood at the Alfred P. Sloan Foundation; Carol Burger, Dawn Pickard, and Ruta Sevo at the National Science Foundation; and the Small Research Grants Program at the Spencer Foundation—have made the projects reported here and the writing of the book itself possible.

We are especially grateful to the students, both women and men, who gave of their time and confidences in our study. We hope they will find their stories accurately and meaningfully reported here. We are also grateful to the hundreds of high school teachers who have shared their time and expertise with us.

Finally, we are pleased to acknowledge our families. Jane's parents, Jules and Doris Margolis, and Allan's mother, Amy Fisher, have lent their support. Jane's husband, Mark, and Allan's wife, Eden, have been outstanding readers of multiple drafts. Jane's daughter, Sophie, and Allan's children, Clark and Miranda, have not only been patient and supportive in their own ways but also have lent us additional firsthand insights into our topic.

Unlocking the Clubhouse

Introduction: Women out of the Loop

Maria is a college student majoring in computer science. She tells us about her first semester in college and her feeling that her male peers know much more than she does about computing:

I keep reminding myself, "You have only been here a month. Give yourself some time, and you will learn something." Meanwhile, I am sitting here thinking, "How come they know how to do this, but I don't know how to do this? . . . I should have been prepared at the same rate they were."

Maria says that when she asks her male peers how they already know so much about computing, they say, "Oh, we learned all of this on our own, years ago. We have been programming like this for ages." Maria "tries not to be jealous."

Another student, Rebecca, tells us how her family got a computer when she was quite young and how she watched her older brother, who "just totally took to it." She began to wonder, "What is this thing?" Her brother would "play little games on it, little stupid games," and sometimes he took the computer apart: "he'd take it apart and tinker with something, and he'd put it back together . . . and it would work again. And I always thought it was pretty interesting." Rebecca never learned to program the computer and never tinkered with the machine, as her brother did: "I never pulled them apart, said, 'Oh, I wonder what this does.' For whatever reason, I never did. He always did."

Maria and Rebecca are two of the more than 100 college students we interviewed over a period of four years—from 1995 to 1999. These two women are part of the forefront of information technology, but already they feel its male dominance.

Amid the tumultuous changes technology is making in the way we live our personal and professional lives, women and girls are out of the computer science loop. At the turn of the century, women are surfing the web in equal proportion to men, and women make up a majority of Internet consumers. Yet few women are learning how to invent, create, and design computer technology. In the nation's research departments of computer science, fewer than 20 percent of the graduates are female. Fewer still enroll in high school programming or advanced computer science classes. Despite the relative youth of the computer industry, much of which has developed since the rise of the women's movement, women have lost ground in the world of computing. As featured in a thirty-year-old children's book titled *I'm Glad I'm a Boy! I'm Glad I'm a Girl!*, the gender distinction "boys invent things and girls use things that boys invent" remains uncomfortably true today.

Why should it matter if the inventors, designers, and creators of computer technology are mostly male? At the most basic and individual level, girls and women who have the necessary talent and inclination but do not become engaged in the technology are missing the educational and economic opportunities that are falling into the laps of computer-savvy young men. Computing salaries are high, jobs plentiful, and entrepreneurship opportunities unbounded. Furthermore, a command of information technology is an asset in many contexts outside the field itself. Since so many facets of education and the economy are driven by technology, an understanding of the workings "under the hood" can be invaluable.

The stakes are high for the national economy as well. The information technology profession, by most accounts, is in the midst of a severe workforce shortage; it is estimated that more than 900,000 jobs are unfilled. One survey of software projects found that 40 percent had been canceled and another 35 percent had serious problems, with much of the difficulty attributed to a shortage of skilled workers. The cost to the economy of this labor shortage has been estimated at $3 billion to $4 billion per year in Silicon Valley alone. Yet every day, talented girls and women who could fill these gaps are disaffected or discouraged from pursuing computing careers.

In the long run, the greatest impact may be on the health of computing as a discipline and its influence on society. The near absence of women's voices at the drawing board has pervasive effects. Workplace systems are built around male cultural models, and entertainment software fulfills primarily male desires. In a particularly poignant example, some early voice-recognition systems were calibrated to typical male voices. As a result, women's voices were literally unheard. Similarly, some early video conferencing systems, in which the camera automatically focused on the speaker, ignored the participation of women. If women could not be heard, they could not be seen. These examples show how a product-design group that is not representative of its users can go wrong. Similar cases are found in many other industries. For instance, a predominantly male group of engineers tailored the first generation of automotive airbags to adult male bodies, resulting in avoidable deaths for women and children. A mostly male group of engineers designed artificial heart valves sized to the male heart. Women must be part of the design teams who are reshaping the world, if the reshaped world is to fit women as well as men.

Along with technology's power come responsibilities to determine what computing is used for and how it is used. These concerns may not be on the mind of adolescent boys who get turned on to computing at an early age and go on to become the world's computer wizards. But these concerns must be part of a computer scientist's line of work. The conversation among computer scientists should not be isolated to all-boy clubhouses; women's voices and perspectives should be part of this conversation. For this to happen, women must know more than how to *use* technology; they must know how to design and create it.

The Evidence

This book reports on our multiyear project to understand and improve the situation of women in computer science education, primarily at the college level but also at the elementary and secondary levels. We set out to understand the different ways men and women approach and experience computing in college and beforehand. We wanted to understand the daily experiences of women studying computer science, capture the dynamics and details of the "leaky pipeline"—the exodus of women from computer science—and develop ways of increasing women's participation (Camp, 1997).

In this book, we lay out the blueprints—the doors, walls, and windows—of the "boys' clubhouse" of computing education. We show how rarely girls' interest in computing is kindled and how women who do develop an interest in computing often have it extinguished in school.

We discuss what is necessary to remodel education so that girls and women who are or could be interested in computing can find a home in the discipline.

The foundation of our analysis is more than 230 interviews conducted with over 100 male and female computer science students over four years (from 1995 to 1999) at Carnegie Mellon University, home to one of the premier computer science departments in the country. During this time Allan, a computer scientist, was associate dean for undergraduate education at the School of Computer Science, while Jane, a social scientist focused on gender and education, was a visiting research scientist at the school. Our research team conducted multiple interviews with male and female students about their early experiences with computers, their home and school environments, their personal and computing interests, their decisions to study computer science, and their undergraduate experiences. Through these conversations, observations of classrooms, discussions with faculty, and comparisons of our data with a growing body of research on the topic, we found a multifold series of influences contributing to the computing gender gap.

Very early in life, computing is claimed as male territory. At each step from early childhood through college, computing is both actively claimed as "guy stuff" by boys and men and passively ceded by girls and women. The claiming is largely the work of a culture and society that links interest and success with computers to boys and men. Curriculum, teachers' expectations, and culture reflect boys' pathways into computing, accepting assumptions of male excellence and women's deficiencies in the field. There is also a subset of boys and men who burn with a passion for computers and computing. Through the intensity of their interest, they both mark the field as male and enshrine in its culture their preferences for single-minded intensity and a focus on technology. We found that these influences express themselves in a variety of ways at different stages of life—hence the developmental framework of our book.

The corresponding process of women ceding the field, largely through disinterest and disaffection, is also complex. Careful observation shows that disinterest and disaffection are neither genetic nor accidental nor inherent to the field but are the bitter fruit of many external influences. By the time they finish college, most women studying computer science have faced a technical culture whose values often do not match their own and have encountered a variety of discouraging experiences with teachers, peers, and curriculum. Many end up doubting their basic intelligence and their fitness to pursue computing. One woman student viewed her misfit with the prevailing culture this way:

> When I have free time, I don't spend it reading machine learning books or robotics books like these other guys here. It's like, "Oh, my gosh, this isn't for me." It's their hobby. They all start reading machine learning books or robotics books or build a little robot or something, and I'm not like that at all. In my free time, I prefer to read a good fiction book or learn how to do photography or something different, whereas that's their hobby, it's their work, it's their one goal. I'm just not like that at all. I don't dream in code like they do.

"Dreaming in code" has become one of our working metaphors, emblematic of a male standard of behavior in this computer-oriented world.

Outline of the Book

To more comprehensively understand the male claim on the field and the erosion of girls' and women's interest in computing, we found ourselves looking back from college to the earliest roots of gender socialization. Chapter 1, The Magnetic Attraction, is based on college students' accounts of their first attachments to computers. Triangulating these observations with results from the literature of childhood gender development, this chapter examines how gender socialization in the home sets in motion boys' claim to the computer. Chapter 2 discusses how the convergence of adolescence, peer relationships, computer game design, and secondary schooling helps further boys' claim to and girls' retreat from computing.

Chapter 3, Computing with a Purpose, begins our examination of women's experiences in college computer science. In this chapter we discuss the interests of women majoring in computer science and how their orientation toward and concerns about computing are different from what is offered in most computer science curricula. The next two chapters describe the processes whereby women who were enthusiastic about computing find their confidence and interest extinguished in the college years. Chapter 4, on Geek Mythology, talks about women's alienation and resistance to the norms of "geek culture." Chapter 5 discusses how women's confidence in this male-dominated field diminishes over time and how drops in confidence precede drops in interest. In chapter 6 we present some counterintuitive stories of women's persistence that refute the fallacies that contribute to male claiming and female retreat. Many of these stories of achievement reveal the promise and the pleasures the computing field can hold for women.

In chapters 7 and 8 we present stories of educational change, both in high schools and in universities. We focus on two stories that have deeply engaged us. The first, described in chapter 7, describes a program we designed with colleagues and during which we worked with 240 high school computer science teachers from around the country in an effort to recruit and retain more girls in their courses. Many of these teachers are now active and effective agents of change in their classes, engaging increasing numbers of the next generation's computing experts and encouraging their female students to pursue college majors in computer science.

The second story, in chapter 8, involves the impact of our research at the university level. A variety of formal and informal changes have been and are being made at Carnegie Mellon University, ranging from the design of the curriculum to the education of teaching assistants to the way the university thinks about admissions. Five years after we began interviewing the seven women in a class of ninety-six (7 percent), both the size of the entering class and the proportion of women entering the program have increased. In the fall of 2000, fifty-four of 130 entering students (42 percent) were women. In this chapter, we discuss how this happened.

The study of computer science education can be seen as a microcosm of how a realm of power can be claimed by one group of people, relegating others to outsiders. While not ruling out the possibilities of gender differences in cognitive preferences, we challenge the assumption that computer science is "just boring for girls and women" by showing the weighty influences that steal women's interest in computer science away from them. Our book tells the story of women students who were once enthusiastic about studying computer science and what happens to them in schools. We describe what teachers and parents need to do to engage and protect girls' interests and change computer science into a field that is engaging and interesting for a much larger and more diverse group of students. The goal is not to fit women into computer science as it is currently taught and conceived. Rather, a cultural and curricular revolution is required to change computer science so that the valuable contributions and perspectives of women are respected within the discipline.

The Site of Our Investigation

The site of our investigation is the Carnegie Mellon School of Computer Science (SCS). If computer technology is giving birth to a new world order, this school is an incubator. Although Carnegie Mellon has less national name recognition than the Massachusetts Institute of Technology or Stanford University, within computing fields it rivals them. The Carnegie Mellon School of Computer Science is generally ranked as one of the best in the world. Growing out of the department founded in 1965 by Herbert Simon, Allen Newell (considered two of the founding fathers of artificial intelligence), and Alan Perlis, SCS has leadership roles in both research and education. It features an array of nationally prominent graduate programs as well as a bachelor's degree program. This latter program, also ranked as one of the best in the world, had been male-dominated from its inception in 1988 up until the beginning of our study in 1995, at which time its enrollment was approximately 8 percent female.

Students' Accounts at the Heart of Our Investigation

From 1995 to 1999 we conducted multiple interviews with fifty-one female and forty-six male computer science undergraduates, along with thirty nonmajors. We interviewed some of the students every semester from their first year all the way through to graduation. Others we interviewed up until they made their decision to leave the major, usually in their sophomore year.

Students' accounts of their experiences, interests, and decisions lie at the heart of our investigation. These longitudinal interviews have allowed us to see more than just snapshots of students' lives at single points in time; the multiple interviews let us observe the evolution of their relationship with the field of computing, through many layers of experience. Our subjects—being the live creatures they are—change and transform in response to their own inner workings and to their environment. We learned that an interview with a student could differ dramatically from her last one. The first interview with a student might find her overflowing with enthusiasm about computing and how much she loves programming. A semester later her confidence might be shaky as she worries about how little she really knows about computing, while everyone else seems to understand so much more. In a third interview she might have found renewed hope in her ability to do well and seem to have figured out what she wants to do in computer science. By the fourth interview she may announce to us that she is leaving the program, having concluded that she just isn't interested in computer science. At any point along the way, had we drawn conclusions prematurely about this student, we would have an incomplete and possibly a misleading story.

As we turned thousands of pages of interview text into chapters, we worked hard to keep students' stories whole. We were careful not to take quotes out of context. We analyzed across interviews by themes and categories. In addition to interviews with computer science majors, we also collected information using classroom observations, surveys of incoming classes, informal interviews with computer science faculty and graduate students, computer science online bulletin-boards, student journals, and a focus group.

A study based on nonquantitative data necessarily raises the question of how conclusions are to be drawn, especially among readers who, like Allan, have grown up with engineering and "hard" science. To the reader who may question our data as "just anecdotes," we provide an explanation offered by Elaine Seymour and Nancy Hewitt (1997), two researchers whose cross-institutional study of why students leave math and science, *Talking About Leaving: Why Undergraduates Leave the Sciences,* was an invaluable source of inspiration for us. They discuss their use of qualitative data and refute the charge that their data are "mere anecdotes":

> We sometimes encounter the objection that the state of affairs collectively portrayed in students' accounts is based on "anecdotal" evidence. Strictly speaking (from its Greek roots), an "anecdote" is an unpublished account. In more general usage, it is a story which is casually heard and has no coherent, patterned connection to other stories on the same theme. By either usage, the accounts which form the text data for this study are not anecdotes. Accounts which are gathered and analyzed in a systematic manner allow the investigator to discover things that cannot easily be discovered by any other means. In complex human affairs, noticing the patterns in the independent accounts of expert witnesses plays the same role as laboratory observations in the formation of hypotheses. As the reader will perhaps concede, there is much to be learned by treating such accounts with respect. (p. 396)

We also have found that by labeling interview transcripts according to the patterns of issues that arise, it is also possible to extract quantitative observations from qualitative data. This issue is discussed further in the appendix on research methodology.

What about the challenge that students' accounts are a self-serving rewriting of history that allows them to "save face" or to construct a story that makes sense to themselves, their parents, and their peers? Wendy Luttrell (1997), in her book *School-smart and Mother-wise: Working-Class Women's Identity and Schooling,* regards the women's stories she gathered as "accounts," which as in a mathematical model "must add up" for each woman as she interprets what she experiences. In Luttrell's view, as in ours, these accounts "could be said to provide them a means to reconcile their past experiences, feelings, and self-understandings in school with their current lives" (p. 4). And while Luttrell concedes that these accounts may be "partial," they also "provide important insights into the conditions shaping the women's lives" (p. 4).

We have worked to listen carefully to students' accounts of their experiences and translate them in ways that are both accurate and useful for conveying how the gender gap in computer science perpetuates itself. We have learned that we cannot think in terms of a static set of influences on students' experiences but rather must understand students' stories in terms of a web of influences and a sequence of turning points, at each of which a different set of factors may be critical.

While Carnegie Mellon is particularly competitive and selective, we believe our findings to be transferable to other settings. Still, we recommend that other institutions embark on their own studies of their experiences with female computer science students. This research was a living part of Carnegie Mellon for four years and became a real impetus for institutional change. Faculty and administrators who had not given much thought to this issue began to do so. It is tempting for a community to think "that is not us" unless the data come from its own back yard.

Gender Generalizations

It is all too easy to fall into thinking that "women are this way and men are that way"—to simplify the categories and underplay all the contradictions and differences within each individual and within each gender. At the same time, it is misleading to see women as sharing no unifying experiences. Feminist theorist Ruth Behar (1993) warns that the "opposite tendencies to see women as not all different from one another or as all too different" can lead one to go too far in either direction and then end up indifferent (p. 301). Wendy Luttrell (1997) adds that going too far in either direction can lead one to disconnect, to be "unconnected to the lives of other women" (p. xiv). Throughout our study, we have worked hard to capture both gender differences and also the wide range of often contradictory experiences women have.

The students we interviewed were predominantly white, Asian American, or international students primarily from Asia, India, and Eastern Europe. Among the fifty-one computer science women students in our sample were twenty-four European Americans, sixteen international students, eight Asian Americans, and three African Americans. Among the forty-six men were twenty-eight European Americans, seven international students, six African Americans, and five Hispanics. The underrepresentation of African American and Hispanic students in our sample reflects the small numbers majoring in computer science. The Computing Research Association Taulbee surveys reveal that such low numbers are pervasive. Among the 2000 recipients of computer science bachelor's degrees from Ph.D.-granting institutions in the United States and Canada, only 4 percent were African American and 3 percent Hispanic. The 1999 Advanced Placement College Board Summary Report statistics show that African American and Hispanic students together make up less than 7 percent of high school advanced placement computer science test-takers nationwide.

While we were conducting our research, we made every effort to learn as much as we could about the underrepresented African American and Hispanic students' experiences. We chronicled their experiences and reported their high attrition rate. But because of the meager numbers of minority students enrolled in computer science classes at Carnegie Mellon, we were not able to analyze systematically the influence of race on students' experiences. Therefore, we do not disaggregate students beyond the issue of gender, except when we consider the situation of international students. This means that almost every student quoted in our book is European or Asian American unless otherwise specified.

The shortage of people of color in the computing profession is even more dire than the shortage of women. All of the reasons we have cited for increasing the participation of women in computing are at least as compelling in the case of ethnic minorities. We hope our investigation of gender and computing can contribute insights and methodological models to efforts to bring an end to the digital divide in the creation and control of information systems.

Our "Insider-Outsider" Collaboration

We were introduced by Barbara Lazarus, the associate provost of Carnegie Mellon, in 1994. She knew that Allan, who was then the associate dean for undergraduate computer science education, was concerned about the scarcity of women studying computer science. She knew that Jane's expertise was in gender and education. Barbara saw the potential for an unusual interdisciplinary collaboration. As soon as we discovered our common beliefs that the absence of women in computer science has large societal implications and that women's absence is also a social justice issue, we were eager to venture forth into previously unknown territory and work together to understand the living dynamics of this multifaceted problem.

As we began our research, we referred to our collaboration as an "insider-outsider" model; at its conclusion, there was no longer any insider or outsider. By interweaving our two perspectives—Jane's expertise in gender, feminism, and education and Allan's expertise in computer science and education—we have attained a more layered understanding of the gender gap in computer science than we had without each other's perspective. Each of us had key pieces of the puzzle that the other lacked. Our collaboration has allowed us to make vital connections—between insider knowledge of computing and its culture and an outsider's ability to see the unseen, between an emphasis on rigor and an ear for nuance, between quantitative knowledge and qualitative knowledge, and between an academic understanding of gender inequalities in our society and the daily experience of those inequalities. Looking at the problem from different perspectives has allowed us to see things that we would otherwise have missed.

This project brings together many strands of our own lives. From 1973 to 1979, Jane worked as a telephone installer, one of the first women to hold that job in San Francisco. She has experienced firsthand how certain knowledge (such as working with tools and understanding electric wiring schemes) is often viewed as inaccessible by women. She experienced firsthand what it felt like to lack the "physical intuition" that the males around her had for working with tools and wiring. She was shocked at how easy it was to learn the necessary skills with a little bit of "affirmative action" training. Working as an installer was a life-transforming experience, but when Jane left the job, she quickly reverted back to a state of dread whenever a new form of technology was introduced. The social conditioning many girls receive as children runs very deep, and it takes a lot to uproot it.

In 1985, Jane enrolled in graduate school and studied gender and education at the Harvard Graduate School of Education with feminist Carol Gilligan. For her dissertation she researched women's experiences in the Department of Government classrooms at Harvard—how women questioned their own intelligence within a very male-dominated culture. Her next project was the topic of this book.

For Allan, beginning this project was a natural extension of his interest in enhancing access to computing careers. His first leadership role in education at Carnegie Mellon involved the creation of an undergraduate program in a department that previously had educated only Ph.D. students; this led over time to a tenfold increase in the number of degrees granted. The same motivation led him to design the high school teacher program discussed in chapter 7, as well as to co-found a new organization, Carnegie Technology Education. Carnegie Technology Education, which Allan now heads, is a Carnegie Mellon subsidiary that builds and supports web-based courses in software development for the use of other organizations, primarily educational institutions such as community colleges. The focus is to provide a large and diverse student body with access to high-quality, up-to-date curricula delivered by appropriate and supportive local instruction.

Boys Invent Things, and Girls Use Things Boys Invent

Today, the world of cyberspace is shaping our environment and our culture. Very little is unaffected by the onslaught of technology. The actual products of computer science change the way we do business, the interaction we expect from work, life, and pleasure, and the way we regard entertainment. If *boys invent things, and girls use things boys invent,* a cyberspace culture will inevitably reflect the desires and sensibilities of males to the exclusion and often denigration of females.

We began working on the gender gap in computer science in 1994 and have been committed to producing more than a report that sits on a shelf. We hope that teachers at all levels, parents, students, computer industry folks, and readers of all types who are interested in processes of gender socialization and the new world of computer technology will be among our readers. We hope our research will spark conversations on why so few girls and women study computer science, how early gender socialization and schooling constrict the options of many girls, and what women can add to the world of computing.

1

The Magnetic Attraction

The following is a journal entry written by Jane after dropping off her daughter at her kindergarten:

Each morning as I walk my daughter into her classroom, I am struck by the gender divide that greets us: boys huddled around the computers (sometimes two rows deep with boys looking over the shoulders of their friends) and girls squeezed around the art table or falling all over each other on the reading couch.

When I point this out to the teacher, she shakes her head, acknowledging that she also sees what I see. "It's a self-selection issue. This is where the kids choose to go." She tells me how even one of the girl "computer consultants" (the first-graders who are allowed to turn on the machines for the kindergarten kids) does not spend her free time at a computer after turning them on in the morning.

Another detail of this scene catches my attention: there are two idle computers. Boys are not hogging all the computers, using sharp elbows to push the girls off. The girls remain on the couch despite the free computers.

How do these children make their decisions about where to go first thing in the morning? Is it individual preference or a group dynamic? Do the kids sense a "boy side" of the room and a "girl side" of the room? If so, is it mere coincidence that computers are on the "boy side"? Has the computer row become the new block corner where boys "voluntarily" congregate and girls are rarely seen? Are parents and teachers unconsciously guiding their daughters and sons to their respective corners? When does this all begin? These kids are only five and six years old!

As early as kindergarten, girls use the computer eagerly and skillfully for writing their stories, but boys race to the computers for free time and play. Many kindergarten children in America daily play out the scene Jane describes. Parents scratch their heads in puzzlement as to how this has come about. Many parents describe their homes as places where sons and daughters are treated equally. Yet they also wonder about what feels like a gravitational pull between their children and certain toys and activities that seems to override notions of gender neutrality. The computer now gets added to the list of blocks, cars, chess sets, and other things that boys play with most and is absent from the list of girls' favorites.

Boys' and girls' relationships to computers revisit some of the thorniest questions of gender. Why are boys enthralled and girls lukewarm? And why do these differences appear so early? Why do many more young boys than girls play with toys that introduce children to mechanical and visual spatial skills, such as Legos, chess, and now computers? It is not that girls are not interested in computers. They are. There are plenty of fights between brothers and sisters over who has the mouse and which game to play. But quite early an involvement and connection develops between many boys and the computer that is more intense and all-consuming than it is for most girls. Many more boys than girls get inside the machine and become tinkerers. They learn it inside and out, whereas more girls stay on the outside and limit their involvement.

Despite the rapid changes in technology and some fifteen years of literature covering the era of the ubiquitous personal computer, a remarkably consistent picture emerges: more boys than girls experience an early passionate attachment to computers, whereas for most girls attachment is muted and is "one interest among many." These attachment differences help to shape students', parents', and teachers' expectations that boys and men, *not* girls and women, will excel in and enjoy computing.

Boys and Computers: The Magnetic Attraction

As we sit across from more than a hundred enthusiastic male and female computer science students, listening to them talk about their histories and experiences with computers, most of the men describe an early, sizzling attraction to the computer. It is as if they fell in love at first sight, and from then on they knew that this would be something they would like to spend the rest of their lives doing.

Henry, a first-year computer science student, recounts how he loved computers "probably too much . . . you know, radiation burns on my face. You know what I mean? I liked computers a lot." When he was in the sixth grade, his dad borrowed a computer from a friend. Henry describes the computer as "an old black and white Macintosh, just a totally self-contained one-unit thing." Henry remembers "just playing with that all the time and trying to figure stuff on it. And that got me really hooked."

Then his family bought their first family machine, a 386-16:
plored with that. I learned how to use DOS, and I was really getting ...
figuring things out on computers. And I just knew that that was going to be
something for me."

Larry, an eighteen-year-old student in his first semester studying computer science, recalls how he "got hooked." The words he uses over and
over to characterize his relationship to the computer are "fascinating,"
"play," and "fun." The computer became his ultimate plaything. Larry
says, "So I got a 486 then, and that's when my interest just—whew!—sky-
rocketed! . . . I just played with the computer, and that was like my big toy,
and that's pretty much how everything happened."

The fun for the male students is not only in using the computer but in
knowing it and having it do what you want it to do. Jeremy says that what
he likes about the computer is "the fact that I could tell it what to do." He
describes the computer as "a giant toy that was there for me to play with in
any way I want." He explains how the computer is play for him:

I just liked sitting in front of a computer. I didn't find it boring. I found it interesting. It was like playing. I mean, why do you go out and play baseball with your
friends? 'Cause it's fun! Why do you sit in front of a computer? 'Cause it's fun! I did
both!

Sam told us how he wanted to know every detail of how the computer
worked:

And ever since the start I was just kind of interested in knowing how it worked, like
on the inside—what all the parts did and how you got from the stream of 1s and 0s
to Space Plus 3 or whatever video game you play. And I just wanted to know all the
details about what was going on inside the computer. . . . I just wanted to know
how they wrote programs, how they put the whole thing together, and I spent a lot
of time figuring that out.

Discovering and exploring the computer are truly epiphanies for many
of these male students. They start programming early. They develop a
sense of familiarity; they tinker on the outside and on the inside, and they
develop a sense of mastery over the machine. They often are introduced by
a parent who is very involved with computers and is able to seed a budding
interest. They are drawn in by games designed to spark and engage boys'
interests.

Women students have a very different early history to tell. For most, the
attraction is more moderate and gradual.

Girls and Computers: "He Was the One Who Was Really into It"

Sally is a successful second-year computer science student. Her first memory of being turned onto computers was when her dad showed her a brochure for the Apple IIs, which had just come out. This happened relatively early for Sally; she was seven at the time. She thought all the colors were "amazing." She remembers saying "Wow, I want one of those." And that Christmas when her grandmother bought her a computer, Sally tells us, "I was caught totally by surprise. I was in love with it. I played with it all day long. Its OS, as near as you can say, was Basic. So I learned Basic. And I had a lot of fun."

But then comes Sally's qualifying statement: "I mean, I didn't spend all my waking hours on it the way some budding hackers might have, but I really enjoyed just messing around." While Sally describes her time at the computer as "fun," playing at it all day long, enjoying "messing around" with it, she qualifies her attachment and describes it as different from the males around her. Many other women students also qualify their attachment to computers. Mary says that her family had a computer when she was little, but "I never really used it that much." She says, "I find myself odd in that sense that I don't really know much about how to work a computer." By this she means she does not know the operating systems and how to program. She states that she was "never the kind of person to sit at the computer and fiddle with things." While some people change their screen background and "change this and that," all of that tinkering "never really appealed to me."

Almost every woman in our study was enthusiastic about learning computer science. We were, after all, interviewing women students in one of the top computer science departments in the country. Among them were girl gamers, girls who were the presidents of their computer clubs, and girls who were on their school computer teams. Yet most came to computer science later, in high school, through being "math and science" students who enjoyed problem solving, doing puzzles, exercising logical thinking skills, or taking a high school programming class. Most did not have the same experience of falling in love at an early age that many boys did. Early exploration into the computer is the exception among the women. Sasha, for example, has a story more typical of what we heard from the men:

I just liked exploring with the computer. I was never someone that would sit down and read the instructions, like a manual or anything; I would just go in and see what I could do, which is probably why the hard drive crashed! That was me. But I just wasn't afraid of the computer, and I'd try to do anything on it. And you know, it was fun. It was just like a love of exploring on the computer—looking for different things and seeing if I could get it to work.

Staying on the Outside

Few of the women students, though, had engaged the machine as deeply as Sasha. Their earliest stories often begin with descriptions of *watching* a father work at the computer or having an older brother show them how he programmed the machine. They watched and became interested but from the sidelines. Recall Rebecca, who reported that

Like my brother, even just a couple of years ago, he started kind of playing on them, pulling them apart. I never did that. I never pulled them apart, said, "Oh, I wonder what this does." For whatever reason, I never did. He always did.

Male students, on the other hand, talk about their "need to know how things worked." Larry referred to his need as "pathological." For Larry, the computer was the ultimate, the "pinnacle" machine to be explored and mastered. He describes how it went from "taking my toys apart, to taking radios apart, to going through all the Radio Shack X-in-1 kits. Like 160, 200, 301, and then finally getting a computer because that was the pinnacle of stuff I didn't understand." About three-quarters of the men in our study fit the profile of someone who was magnetically attracted to computers when they were quite young and spent much of their youth consumed with computing. Among the women, in contrast, only about one-quarter fit the profile.

Overall, the women we interviewed had done less hands-on exploration of the computer than the men. They gave fewer accounts of working beside their fathers and more stories of *watching* from the sidelines. Computing and tinkering had not been their main childhood activities or focus but one interest among several. They liked to do "neat stuff," like playing games, with the computer, but the machine did not become their all-time favorite plaything. Few women described epiphany moments of falling in love with the computer. In fact, most distanced themselves from this type of relationship to computers. What stands out is how often their accounts of their personal histories with computers highlight a male family member as the one who was "really into computers."

Computing Begins at Home

Our research confirms how influential home environments are for students' developing an interest in computer science. Daniel, an eighteen-year-old freshman, remembers his father bringing home "a little minicomputer" from work when Daniel was quite young. He says that his father "basically laid out my life for me" because Daniel took to computers right away and found his life's passion. Daniel describes his youthful relationship to computing: "I was very much into it." His earliest memory is that he would "go around, punch all these little keys and would watch [the computer] draw little triangles." Another male student, who grew up in a single-parent household, told us, "My mother bought me a computer back in Alabama when I was four years old, and I guess ever since it has been me playing video games, thinking 'Wow, how did they do that?' Trying to get it to work."

Becky describes her household as a "family of nerds." Her family got its first computer when she was in kindergarten: "We got a couple more Apples, got a Compaq, got a PC, started upgrading. After the first couple of years at any given time we would have anywhere from three to five computers in the house, all up and running." She feels that her family background gave her ease and comfort with computers, so that working with computers became "natural" for her.

Forty percent of the male students we interviewed and 65 percent of the women came from households in which one or both parents were involved with computing as a hobby or on the job. Parents impart their computer enthusiasm and skills to their children, and through early mastery acquired at home children gain a competence and confidence they carry with them into school.

While upper- and middle-income children in the digital generation are being introduced to the computer at home, long before kindergarten or even preschool, home access and use are far from universal or uniform. According to the 1997 National Telecommunications and Information Administration report "Falling through the Net," in 1997 white households were more than twice as likely (40 percent) to own a computer as were black (19.3 percent) or Hispanic (19.4 percent) households. This divide cut across all income levels, even at incomes higher than $75,000. While the August 2000 report "Falling through the Net: Toward Digital Inclusion" maintains that "groups that have traditionally been digital 'have-nots' are now making dramatic gains" and that "rapid uptake of new technologies is occurring among most groups of Americans," the Executive Summary of the report reveals that while a third of the U.S. population uses the Internet at home, only 16.1 percent of Hispanics and 18.9 percent of blacks do (p. 2).

Children Are Keen Observers

Mike rollerblades into our office to be interviewed. He laughs as he describes his family lore—his dad's obsession with computers:

My dad was into those sort of things. My mom tells me this story that when my sister was born, to celebrate he went out and bought this calculator. It cost like $600 or something back in the mid-70s. It could actually do sine functions. He was all impressed with it because he was an engineer and he knew that he wouldn't have to look up these tables and everything. And my mom couldn't understand that. She still doesn't understand it, and she's like, "Why do we need a hard drive bigger than 40 megabytes?"

Many students recount a computer gender divide in their families. Jesse's father is a professor of computer science, but his mom is "scared of it." Mary, a first-year student, describes how her chemical engineer father bought the new computers as soon as they came out, but her mother "worked part-time and she's very computer illiterate. She knows how to type, do normal jobs like that, nothing very interesting." Another student describes how his electrical engineer father built computers out of assembled parts with his friends in the basement; he describes his mom as a social worker who is "basically computer illiterate, but we keep trying to teach her." He continues, "Well, my father is not very patient in teaching her, but I keep trying to teach her and help her out." The computer-impaired mother is a stock character in many students' stories.

Children are keen observers. They notice whether their mother or father gets into the driver's seat or the passenger side, they notice who is called for when the electric power goes out or plumbing fails, they notice who sends the thank-you cards, and they notice who tinkers with the computer. In the two-parent household, male members of the family are most often the ones who are "really into it." More men buy computer hardware and software. In our sample of ninety-seven computer science majors, 43 percent identified a male family member as very interested in and knowledgeable about computers, while just 8 percent identified a female family expert. In a study of seventy families' computer use in New York, researchers J. B. Giaquinta, J. Bauer, and J. Levin (1993) found males were the "experts," the key decision makers around the computer, and that mothers were particularly estranged from the machine. They discovered that mothers' sense of their competence within their own homes is challenged by the presence of the computer.

Harvard psychologist Jerome Kagan (1964), a prominent scholar of children's temperament and how children view the world, found that children make unsuspecting gender associations to objects of everyday life. Seemingly neutral objects in a school classroom, such as a blackboard, book, page of arithmetic, or school desk, become feminine in the eyes of young children, apparently because children associate these objects with their predominantly female teachers. In a series of experiments with second- and third-grade students in public schools, Kagan noted that girls' identification of these objects as female was more stable than it was for the boys. The implications he suggests are that "the superior academic performance of girls in the primary grades is facilitated by girls' view of school as congruent with their sex role, whereas boys are more ambivalent" (p. 1051).

As children see dads and brothers tinkering with the computer, being the computer experts in the family, playing games on the computer that obviously speak to boys' interests and not girls', there is the likelihood that very young children will identify the computer as a "he" object. The consequences for daughters and sons of identifying the computer as male and of seeing mothers as having low confidence and ability with technology are far-reaching. Daughters of this generation may not have the same fear of the technology that their mothers do, but daughters still are not becoming the tinkerers, the explorers, the experts in the technology.

The Computer in the Boy's Bedroom

During the time of our research, more than half of the male students we interviewed reported owning their own computer or keeping the family computer in their room when they were young. Women students at Carnegie Mellon seldom refer to a computer being bought "for me." In fact just 17 percent of the women, compared to 40 percent of the men, report being given a computer early on. A study from the mid-1980s of a Midwestern high school (Schofield 1995) found that every single boy who hung out in the computer lab during lunch time reported having a computer at home, whereas not a single girl did so (p. 158).

Lily, a second-year student, has a younger brother. As they were growing up, she was the one who was "really into computers" in high school. But the computer was placed in her brother's room. Lily told us how perplexed she was, since both her mother and father had careers in computing and should have known better. Another female student told us how the family computer was literally locked away from her: "[My brother] had his computer in his room, and when I want to use it like play games or something I had to ask. He had a key. He locked it."

In the Giaquinta, Bauer, and Levin (1993) study of families in New York, the researchers found that for over half of the families, the computer's location made it primarily accessible to the father or to a son. They report that in one household, when the father was asked how the computer came to be located in the master bedroom, by his side of the bed, he replied, "That was easy. I paid for it; I bought it. . . . I'm the father, and I make the rules around here" (p. 84). His wife reported that he was the "master of that machine" and suggested that his ownership may have had something to do with her avoidance of "that machine" (p. 84).

The relationship between children's interests and a parent's influence can fly below the radar of parents' perception. One of our colleagues, a long-time scholar of women's history and a tireless activist in the cause to engage more women with math and science, had a sudden flash of recognition when we mentioned the phenomenon of the computer in the boy's bedroom. A look of panic crossed her face. "Oh, we have the computer in Ben's room," she blurted out, "because he is always on it and seems to use it more."

Actually, this is a conundrum that many parents face. They want to raise children of both genders with a full set of options. They believe that both their daughters and sons should know how to use the computer. And yet when it comes to toys, activities, room decorations, and now the computer, they find themselves buying toys they believe their children will enjoy or are clamoring for. Often this results in unintentionally gender-stereotyped decisions, like placing the computer in the son's room because "he is using it more" and "his friends are using it more."

A subtler version of this story happened in Allan's family:

For years, we'd had a computer in a public spot in the house. Both of my children were interested in using it, neither obsessively—but my son was distinctly more interested. When we began to think about getting a computer for my daughter, we weren't sure it would be a great idea: would she really be interested? It turned out, when we did, that she thought it was "better than getting a TV" (apparently the gold standard for gifts) and has made great use of it. Her level of interest simply had not been apparent when her brother's interest dominated the scene.

Father-Son Internships

While many male students describe learning programming and their way around the computer "on their own," a close examination of their stories shows the importance of the initial introduction, enthusiasm, and just the right knowledge imparted by a parent, usually the father. Ralph, whose father repaired for computers and eventually became a network administrator, would bring home computers that he was working on. When his father was done, Ralph would "get to mess with them—play video games on them or just randomly watch him do things" and "that always thrilled me." When the family eventually owned a computer, he "got to the point where I wanted to do something and he [father] would teach me, and eventually I was pretty much running the computer."

Another male student describes how his father got him started in programming:

In sixth grade my dad bought me a TRS-80, and the book came with it—how to write all these programs—and my Dad and I worked most of the way through it. At one point about halfway through he left me on my own, and I continued the rest of the book. Ever since then I've been programming, and I've been interested in programming, itself.

Timothy describes how his father would give him enough information to get started on the computer and then leave him to learn independently, while being available as a resource:

Well, he worked a lot with Quick BASIC. So basically the way it would work is he might show me one or two things, and then I would try to do something, and then it wouldn't work or I couldn't accomplish something, and I'd go ask him what to do, and he would help me then. And then I'd keep on going on my own until I got stuck again. . . . And he'd help me whenever I had a problem, and I sort of went off exploring on my own then.

According to Jeffrey Goldstein (1994), a researcher of children's play, fathers have been shown to play with their sons 50 percent more than they do with their daughters, and fathers also spend more time educating boys in computing. We heard more accounts of parents, usually fathers, who actively engaged sons than parents who engaged daughters; more men than women describe being "introduced" to the computer by a father. When girls do receive encouragement or enthusiasm from parents, it usually occurs later—in the form of encouraging daughters to take computer science in high school, to major in computer science in college, or to consider computer science as a career. The stories we hear of hands-on internships between parents and daughters are rare exceptions.

Play and Gender: Who Chooses the Toys?

When parents place computers in boys' bedrooms and spend more time nurturing their sons' computing interests than their daughters', are they responding to an innate difference in the children's level of interest? Or are their assumptions about the children's interests playing out as self-fulfilling prophecy? This is the nature-nurture debate that captivates the research on children, play, and toys. A collection of essays by researchers in this field, *Toys, Play and Child Development,* addresses this tension. Jeffrey Goldstein (1994) examines whether parents are responding to what feels like a contrasting intrinsic drive within boys and girls by buying them different types of toys or whether parents overlay their own expectations on their children, thereby socializing girls to like dolls and boys to like trucks and now the computer. He presents examples of research on both the nature and nurture sides of the toy debate.

On the nature side, some researchers believe that an internal engine drives boys' and girls' toy choices. Meyer-Bahnburg, Feldman, Cohen, and Ehrhardt (1988) document a relationship between prenatal exposure to synthetic female hormone and a reduction in rough and tumble play of both sexes. Likewise other researchers found that prenatal exposure to high levels of the male hormone androgen, for both boys and girls, led to a greater preference for traditionally male toys at ages three to eight years

(Berenbaum and Hines 1992). Eaton and Enns (1986) contend that a child's choice of toys is strongly shaped by his or her activity level and that a child with a strong need for movement and activity may prefer traditionally masculine toys because they enable highly active play.

On the nurture side of the debate, Harriet Rheingold and Kaye Cook (1975) inventoried the bedrooms of ninety-six middle-class American children between the ages of one and six. They found strong indications of parental influence. While there were similarities—both boys and girls had stuffed animals, for example—boys' rooms contained more toy animals in barns or zoos, as well as objects relating to pace, energy, or time. Girls' rooms contained more dolls. The most dramatic difference was in the number of vehicles owned by the boys (375) compared to the girls (17). No girls had a trailer, wagon, bus, motorcycle, or boat. Only boys had live animals, depots, replicas of heavy equipment, and military toys; only girls had doll houses, stoves, tea sets, and cradles for dolls. One of the researchers connected to the study had observed that girls of eighteen months spent as much time playing with trucks as boys did. The researchers' conclusion was that parents are not purely responding to the so-called innate interests of kids but, over the intervening years, are themselves responsible for the inventory in their children's rooms becoming so gender stereotyped.

On the other hand, in her book *Sex and Cognition,* Simon Fraser University psychologist Doreen Kimura (2000) argues that evidence of external socializing influences does not disprove preexisting cognitive gender differences. She presents evidence linking prenatal events, such as hormonal levels, to toy choices and cognitive patterns. For example, girls diagnosed with a condition in which the adrenal glands produce an excess of androgens (male hormones) "have toy preferences which are strikingly similar to boys" (p. 26). They play less with dolls and more with vehicles than do other girls. Early exposure to androgens has also been found to contribute significantly to higher scores on spatial tasks, and different levels of testosterone are consistently associated with different spatial scores. Kimura plants herself firmly on the nature side of the nature-nurture debate: "We can say with certainty that there are substantial stable sex differences in cognitive functions like spatial rotation ability, mathematical reasoning, and verbal memory; and in motor skills requiring accurate targeting and finger dexterity. . . . Most of these sexually differentiated functions are strongly influenced by early and/or current hormonal environments" (p. 181).

Jane wrote the following journal entry after having coffee with her daughter's first-grade teacher and a father of one of her classmates. They were discussing male and female attraction to computers, and almost in unison they asked Jane: "Well, what about the brain? Aren't there some cognitive differences that account for this?" Immediately, those questions made Jane think of the Legos she'd never bought for her daughter, Sophie. At an early age, Sophie was very competent at following Lego schematics. At age four and five, she would get a boxed kit, open up the instruction booklet, and proceed to build the Lego contraption. She enjoyed them, she stuck with it, she showed a "brain" for it. But, at preschool she never played at the Lego table. Only the boys did. One day Jane asked Sophie why:

> In answer to my question why she doesn't play at the Lego table at preschool, Sophie told me that "the boys take all the cool stuff." The "cool stuff," apparently, are the little antennas, the helmets, the shields, the accessories that bring the structures to life. OK, so what about home where there are no boys to take all the cool stuff? You would think that with this competence that Mark and I would have filled her room with Legos. This, unfortunately, is not the case. Even as a feminist who studies girls and technology and knows how important these early toy choices are, I did not buy Sophie Legos in the same way I buy her rocks for her rock collection. Could it be that I never played with Legos and that I am not that familiar with them? I am sure that plays a part. Could it be that Mark unconsciously minimizes the importance of Legos for his daughter? He is mortified to think so. Could it be that we didn't detect Sophie's passion for Legos? She is competent, but where is the passion? While she follows a schematic with ease, she doesn't clamor for us to buy more, and she doesn't break out on her own and do free designs with the Legos. The Legos never became her toy of choice. Could this be because Mark and I never conveyed unbridled enthusiasm and joy when she played with Legos, the way we jump up and down when she practices the piano or makes a great sketch? Could it be that neither of us has taken the time to show her the endless possibilities, to share our excitement with her? This is the truth: I truly believe that if Sophie were a boy, I would have filled her room with Legos.

After six years of scrutinizing the gender gap in computing, along with many other researchers who are examining gender and learning, we face a complex web of nature and nurture. Stanford biologist Paul Ehrlich (2000), in an article titled "Tangled Skeins of Nature and Nurture," writes:

> The relative contributions of heredity and environment to various human attributes are difficult to specify. They clearly vary from attribute to attribute. So,

although it is informative to state that human nature is the product of genes' inter-action with environments (both internal and external), we usually can say little with precision about the processes that lead to interesting behaviors in adult human beings. We can't partition the responsibility for aggression, altruism, or charisma between DNA and upbringing. In many such cases, trying to separate the contributions of nature and nurture to an attribute is rather like trying to separate the contributions of length and width to the area of a rectangle, which at first glance also seems easy. When you think about it carefully, though, it proves impossible. (p. 89)

Gender and Kindergarten: "It's for Boys" or "It's for Girls"

Vivian Paley, master kindergarten teacher at the University of Chicago's Laboratory School, is one of the nation's preeminent observers and commentators about children's play at the preschool and kindergarten levels. In her book *Boys and Girls: Superheroes in the Doll Corner,* Paley (1984) notes that when children are around three both boys and girls will cook and the policeman dresses the baby. At around four "the superhero clique has formed and the doll corner is becoming a women's room" (p. xi). Then, a great sea change appears to occur at five or six. By age five, when gender awareness is erupting, both genders are keenly aware of whether an activity is a "boy" or "girl" thing to do. All of a sudden there is talk about "the boys did this and the girls did that," colors begin to matter, and the choice of playmates is cut in half. Around four and five is when boys will go to the blocks and build towers, roads, and fantasy worlds for superheroes. They are continuously building and taking apart. Inanimate objects are the objects of fascination. They are interested in speed. Girls will go more often to the doll corner or the art table and focus on creating and recreating familiar domestic scenes such as their houses, parents, siblings, and pets. They are interested in each other, their families, and endless conversations about their lives. In Paley's account of her attempt to rearrange the gender divide in her classroom, she describes this sorting out by gender as: "children watch one another and synchronize their movements. It is the most exciting game in town, though not everyone knows what game is being played" (p. xi).

Gender researchers Eleanor Maccoby and Carol Jacklin (1987) have also chronicled how from age five on, both boys and girls are aware of each other and want to stay within their own groups. The toys they choose must be appropriate for their gender to attract friends to play with them. They are resistant to changing this order. And now the computer has entered the scene. What was once a number-crunching machine for the defense industry has turned into one of the most coveted play objects and educational tools in the schools.

Risk Taking, Gender, and Computing

There is probably no way to know the direction of influence, but it is clear that multiple layers of gender socialization affect students' attraction or detachment from toys and now the computer. Sherry Turkle (1984), a professor at the Massachusetts Institute of Technology who writes about computing and its impact on our psychological lives, believes a key advantage in the world of computer science is to be an "intrepid explorer" who delights in risk taking and forging ahead into the unknown. Much learning goes on just by playing around with the computer, trying things out to see what they do, and digging into the programming and configuration of the system. One can't be fearful of "getting lost" or breaking the computer. Yet boys are raised to take risks and are expected to be adventurous and bold, while girls are encouraged to be more cautious and careful.

A study by psychologists John Newson and Elizabeth Newson (1968) of four-year-olds and their mothers, is referred to as the "roaming radius study." Researchers measured the distance on the playground mothers allowed their children to wander off before they were called back. They found that girls were regularly called back before they had a chance to roam very far, often with verbal and body language that implied they face danger if they are far from their mothers; boys were allowed to explore much further. In the late 1970s, researchers found that in the course of an afternoon's play, a typical ten- or twelve-year-old boy may travel a distance of 2,452 yards, while the average girl of the same age might travel only 959 yards. These types of influences recur throughout a child's life, with the result that hesitancy and risk avoidance appears more "innate" in girls than in boys.

The classic psychological studies, known as the Baby X studies, examined how adults respond differently to infants depending on the child's gender. One such study, by John Condry and Sandra Condry (1976), had subjects watching a videotape of a nine-month-old baby reacting to several emotionally stimulating toys, such as a teddy bear, a toll, a buzzer, and a jack-in-the-box. Half of the subjects were told the child was a boy, and the other half were told the child was a girl. When the "boy" infant cried in response to the jack-in-the-box, subjects interpreted it as anger. When the "girl" infant cried in response to the same toy, subjects interpreted it as fear. Over time, as adults label children's emotional responses, the children begin to see themselves in these terms. Without a sense of ability and confidence, interest in exploring can be thwarted.

How a Girl Is Supposed to Be

A second-year student, Suzanne, looks back on her family, her childhood, and her early years with the computer. She regrets how little hands-on experience she had. She says, "I think I wish I did pull apart a computer more than I did." She says she found it difficult to hang around with kids who were doing that because of her family expectations of what activities should interest a female. She describes her family's attitude as "you're not supposed to be interested in that type of thing, and that shouldn't be so important or interesting to you":

I think maybe because it's primarily thought of as a male field, even in my family itself. The women kind of do women-type things and the men kind of do technical-type things. I found it difficult trying to be a girl and also be technical at the same time. I had to pick between the way my family kind of separates between male and female. I had to pick between if I wanted to talk about cooking or recipes or that type of thing or if I wanted to go with the guys and pull apart a computer because I did do that.

Suzanne felt torn between her interests and how the world expected her to be. She felt lonely out there as the exception to the rule—a girl interested in technical things.

Carole tells us about her father, who wouldn't let her touch the machine to get the hands-on experience she so much wanted. She says her father was "always the maintainer of our computer." If he ever did agree to show her something on the computer, "it would be like, 'OK I'll do it and you watch.'" She found this frustrating because she feels she learns better through hands-on experience than by watching someone else do something. Her vow to herself: "In ten years when I have my children . . . , I definitely want to expose her, if I had a daughter, to the technical—I mean, give her little army men to play with or whatever or buy her a chemistry set or a chess set instead of just dolls." Carole's story is consistent with national trends, according to the 1992 American Association of University Women report *How Schools Shortchange Girls.* Its authors report that by third grade 51 percent of boys but only 37 percent of girls have used microscopes and that by eleventh grade 49 percent of boys but only 17 percent of girls have used electricity meters. While we can imagine that there are fathers in the world who will not let their sons touch their computers either, we heard no similar stories from male students.

The Lucky Exceptions

Despite the array of family dynamics that dampen girls' interest in computing, our research also shows what happens in the cases of the lucky exceptions. Kathryn, for example, grew up with her father and brother. She considers herself "lucky" because both her father and brother were "computer geeks" who expected her to participate right along with them:

I must be lucky just because I lived with my brother and my dad for the longest time, and both of them are computer geeks, and they're just kind of like, "Oh, well you should be a computer geek too. Hey, if you're going to act all fuzzy like a chick and all, we're just not going to talk to you." Well, that's what my brother was like. My brother loved the fact that I would stay up 'till three in the morning playing Street Fighter II with him. My brother was like, "My sister is so cool because she . . ." And I don't think a lot of other people get that. I think a lot of people get the . . . "Oh, computers. . . . My brother stays up all night being a geek and playing Diablo. I'm not like that. I don't care about computers."

Another student, Vera, says that she always had a computer in her house, and "you never had the feeling that 'you can't do that, you are a girl.' " Vera told us that her mother, who is a doctor, would always buy her three daughters the "guy" toys like Legos and transformers because "she actually liked to play with that stuff herself." Currently, all three sisters are in college and interested in the sciences.

Summary

As students, parents, and teachers look around and see some boys' overt "magnetic attraction" to computers, they develop expectations about who will (and who will not) succeed in computer science. Parents' and teachers' expectations and assumptions have weighty influence on the choices of children. It is therefore critically important to deconstruct all that lies behind boys' magnetic attraction to computers.

Sheila Tobias (Alper, 1993), in her study of women in science, argues that the "boy wonder icon"—the association of male traits (such as starting very early in life with an obsessive focus) with success in science—is central to the male-biased assumptions and expectations of who does (and who does not) become a scientist. In her article "The pipeline is leaking women all the way," Tobias explains:

One of the characteristics of the ideology of science is that science is a calling, something that a scientist wants to do, needs to do above all else and at all costs. Another is that both scientific talent and interest come early in life—the boy wonder syndrome. If you don't ask for a chemistry set and master it by the time you are five, you won't be a good scientist. Since far fewer girls and women display these traits than boys and men, you end up with a culture that discriminates by gender. (p. 411)

Childhood behaviors, however conditioned by gender socialization and genetics, tend to set computing on the male side of the gender divide. In the next chapter, we show how these issues are compounded by what happens during adolescence in precollege computer science education.

2

Middle and High School: A Room of His Own

In secondary schools across the nation, a repeated pattern plays out: a further increase in boys' confidence, status, and expertise in computing and a decline in the interest and confidence of girls. Curriculum, computer games, adolescent culture, friendship patterns, peer relations, and identity questions such as "who am I ?" and "what am I good at?" compound this issue. Games propel boys, at an early age, into the world of computing and reinforce a general belief that computing is a male activity. Teachers, guidance counselors, parents, and students expect "boy wonders" to be interested in and good at computing. Computer science curriculum has traditionally reflected boys' interests and experience levels. School computers and computing centers have been claimed as the territory of a subset of male students who are the school's computing experts. And girls, as "outsiders," do not see how they and what they value can fit into the computer culture and curriculum.

"It's the Same Boys All the Time"

Corina Koch (1995), a teacher at a predominantly white middle-class school in Kingston, Ontario, observed the interactions of girls in the seventh and eight grades with computers in their classrooms. In math classes, she found that girls were not at the computer. They spent their time polishing the neatness and detail of their work or practicing to improve their math performance. During technology class girls would help other female students with their projects rather than spend their free time at the computer. Koch was interested in what appeared to be girls' tendency to opt out of computer use during classroom "free time." Boys, on the other hand, were always at the computer.

Koch asked the girls why they were not using the computer. They told her that they "didn't use them because the boys did" and because "boys always get there first"—the "same boys all the time" (p. 6). The girls told Koch that "the same boys" who gathered in the computer room to use the computers during lunch also had a computer "recess club" that named the computers "Pubert," "Enzo," "Big G," and "X-Con" (p. 9). The girls not only disliked the names but also objected to the process of naming. They felt that the whole class and not just the boys in the "recess club" should have named the computers. Koch observed how much of boys' free time and boys' friendships often took place around the computer and how "boy culture was fused seamlessly with computer use" (p. 7). And she saw how girls stayed away.

"Kid culture"—as identified by Kathleen McDonnell in her book *Kid Culture: Children & Adults & Popular Culture* is a phenomenon that "remains stubbornly sex-segregated" (p. 45); this culture helps to cement this gender-divided arrangement around the computers in the schools. Instead of allowing students to use the computers during free time on a first-come first-serve basis—a situation that boys dominated—Koch found it necessary to have computer time assigned. Unless the teacher specifically assigned girls their time at the computer, the computers were appropriated by the boys.

Through Koch's own experience of trying to learn a computer game, she also realized how important communal learning, community, and shared knowledge was for computer learning. Boys often formed friendship communities around shared experience and knowledge around the computer. Girls rarely formed these computing communities and thus missed out on a critical source of learning.

High School Computing Lab: A Room of His Own

From 1985 to 1987, a research team conducted observations in the school computer lab in a large, urban, mid-western high school. Janet Schofield (1995), a professor of social psychology at the University of Pittsburgh, led the two-year ethnographic study as the school began to use a computerized geometry tutoring system. Gender was not on her radar when she began the research, but it quickly emerged as one of the most salient issues.

Over the two years of the study, a group of predominantly white male students from the gifted program began to hang out in the computer lab during lunch time. The lab was where the school's computers were concentrated, and it was open during lunch hour for students' use. One student described these regulars as "the revenge of the nerds . . . the kind of person . . . who wouldn't go out. . . . they would rather sit at home playing games on the computer, typing programs" (p. 146). The lab functioned for these students as a retreat from the "hurly burly of the cafeteria, where jocks and the social set rule" (p. 147). These boys were not the jocks or part of the social scene; they were the "brainiacs" of the school, often socially awkward. The lab became "a room of his own" where these students could be smart and be free to be who they were. It was an important sanctuary for these kids at a time when the dominant high school culture is obsessively concerned with appearance over substance and it is often "uncool" for boys as well as girls to be too smart. During their lab lunch, the regulars played competitive computer games and talked about computers. Often these students knew much more about the computers than the teacher on duty and helped troubleshoot anything that went wrong. The researchers observed that in the lab these boys seemed to develop their sense of place, belonging, and friendship. Schofield believes that the lab "provided a context in which these boys were able to build friendships and enact behaviors that supported a positive traditionally masculine image of themselves" (p. 147). They staked their claim on the lab space, and it stuck.

Schofield and her team of researchers observed what happened when anyone from outside of this group entered the high school computer lab. They witnessed several incidents when male African American students came into the lab. Usually these students were ignored, stood around, watched awhile, and then left. Neither the other students nor even the teacher invited them to join them at the computers. The few girls who came into the lab generally came to use the computers for a specific purpose, not to play games or hang out. Playing computer games and using the computer more generally were seen by some girls as a way that "boys filled up the void in their lives left by the difficulties they faced in forming meaningful friendships" (p. 155).

Researchers also observed the more advanced computer science classes, where only one or two girls were enrolled. Schofield notes that harassment of girls in Computer Science 2 classes stood out from the very large number of other classes she observed. Girls were perpetually teased about their bodies, their appearance, and their competence. The male teacher did not intervene on behalf of the girls. One of the women students asked the teacher why he always used football examples; he replied that she could do the programming assignments on anything she wanted. At that cue, a male student turned to her and mockingly said "Do it on sewing," which drew laughs from the other students. Another woman student used football statistics in her program (similar to everyone else's program). She was ridiculed because she used the name of a baseball team instead of a football team. Two male students were observed playing Concentration and trying to modify it. One of the new prizes was the services of a prostitute who charged $200. There was no teacher response to these incidents. None of the high school girls enrolled in Computer Science 2 went on to enroll in Computer Science 3.

High School Computer Science as an All-Boy Club

Today's typical high school computer science curriculum usually consists of one required introductory course in which students learn basic computing skills, such as keyboarding, Internet access, and file management. This course is often required for all students. More advanced courses are offered as electives, if at all. Whether they are offered depends on such things as whether teachers are ready to teach them, equipment is available, and school administration is supportive. Nationwide, very few girls enroll in the upper-level computer science courses.

In 1998, the American Association of University Women (AAUW) convened a Commission on Technology, Gender, and Teacher Education. The Commission issued its findings in a report entitled *Tech-Savvy: Educating Girls in the New Computer Age* (2000), which discusses the gender divide in the technology-rich learning environment of Fairfax, Virginia public schools (p. 46). In 1999 the Fairfax County Human Relations Advisory Committee issued a report on gender-equity issues that showed the skewed enrollment figures for computer science courses. While more girls than boys were signing up for word processing classes, in the advanced computer science classes enrollment was predominantly male: in the artificial intelligence class, 94 percent of the students were male; in the business computer programming classes, 77 percent were male. The numbers were less skewed in the information systems and the desktop publishing classes, at 54 percent male and 46 percent female. Across the country, a 1999–00 California Basic Educational Data System report showed that 301 male and 88 female Los Angeles unified school district students took an advanced placement computer science class. Nationwide, according to the College Board (1999) advanced placement *Summary Report,* only 17 percent of those taking the advanced placement test in computer science in 1999 were female, making computer science the subject with the smallest proportion of female test takers.

Students, parents, and school counselors often do not understand how students can benefit from studying computer science. It is commonly viewed as a vocational skill, limited to keyboarding or using applications. But for many educators and computer science teachers, students who learn the basic principles of programming and other computer science fundamentals are becoming fluent with information technology. With these skills, students will be in a position to design and create technology and, in the words of the AAUW (2000) report, "apply technology in sophisticated, innovative ways to solve problems across disciplines and subject areas" (p. x). Many computer science teachers argue that computer science involves developing higher-order critical thinking skills and problem-solving skills important for all students, not just those who intend to make a career of computing.

The AAUW Technology Commission also found computer science classes often to be "bastions of poor pedagogy" (p. 41). Assignments and teaching examples often embed male-dominated interests and activities, such as sports statistics and card and number tricks. There is often little in computer science instructional materials to draw in girls. Mae Jemison, an astronaut and one of the AAUW Commissioners, calls for revisioning computer science: "Call it Oceanography, and they will come" (AAUW 2000, p. x). Although computing is integrally linked to critical investigations in medicine, environmental science, famine control, art, and music, computer science textbooks focus primarily on technical detail, with little attention paid to the application and impact of the technology in meaningful interdisciplinary problem-solving assignments.

The Legacy of Math and Science

The common practice of grouping computer science with math and science, both informally and organizationally, may exacerbate the gender gap in computing. Girls' confidence in their math and science abilities remains a serious concern, despite significant strides in their participation and performance in those courses.

Fifteen years ago, high school girls were taking far fewer advanced math and science classes than boys, but by the late 1990s roughly equal numbers of girls and boys took precalculus, trigonometry, and statistics and probability, and with similar success. Similarly, enrollment in science courses has nearly equalized, except in the most advanced physical science courses. Although this enrollment and success gap has been nearly erased, girls still underestimate their math abilities, while boys overestimate theirs.

Years of research by scholars such as Elizabeth Fennema (2000), Jacquelynne Eccles (1989, 1994), and Janet Hyde (Hyde, Fennema, Ryan, and Frost, 1990) have shown that women are significantly less confident than men in their math and science abilities, even when their achievements are equal to those of men. Even when they receive the same grades as men, women are still less secure in their academic performance. Girls in elementary school generally like math, but by high school they are less likely than boys to feel competent in math, despite their higher grades.

Girls who lack confidence in their math abilities are probably less likely to take optional math-related courses, including computer science. Part of the reason for the closing enrollment gap, despite the persistence of the confidence gap, may be that a strong record in math and science is important for college admission. In the absence of that motivation, girls may be less willing to pursue an endeavor in which they lack confidence. For example, to avoid jeopardizing their grade point average, they may opt for courses that are familiar and less competitive.

Test scores on the computer science advanced placement exam also demonstrate a gender gap. The 1999 *Summary Report* from the College Board shows the mean score on the A exam to be 2.91 for males and 2.47 for females. The gender gap in performance on math-related exams such as the SAT math test has been the subject of much research. Among the issues being examined are possible biases in the test problems, differences in test-taking confidence, and aptitude differences for different mathematical tasks.

"Who Am I?" and "What Am I Good At?"

Adolescence is a time of identity formation. Students acquire a sense of themselves as college-bound or not, as strong or weak in certain areas, or as math-science or humanities types. Unfortunately, they too often feel that they must choose between one or the other kind of course. The judgments that teachers and guidance counselors make and the encouragement they give (or not) to take certain courses enormously affects how students see themselves.

Friends also play a role in students' decisions about which courses to take. Classes and groups of kids have reputations. Computer science students' are often associated with being "supersmart" and "nerdy." We interviewed a female high school student who had been identified by her teachers as being computer savvy. In her interview she discusses her concern about becoming too focused on computers, as the boys are:

I guess this sounds kind of funny, but I don't want to be the kind of person who stays up in their room late at night . . . soaking in the rays from the computer and hunched over the keyboard. I just don't like that image, and I want to stay away from that. I mean, I like doing it, but I don't like doing it to extremes. . . . I think it's a stereotype, but I don't think it would have become a stereotype if there weren't some truth to it. I mean, I know people who do this. I know someone who goes to bed early so he can get up in the middle of the night and type on his computer. And that frightens me, you know?

Adolescent Girls, Confidence Loss, and Computer Science

Adolescence is a period of heightened risk and is difficult for everyone, but one of its most dramatic impacts is a drop in girls' sense of confidence and competence. In a 1992 AAUW study, 3,000 boys and girls between nine and fifteen were polled about their attitudes toward self, school, friends, and family. While boys thought they were pretty good at things, girls were more likely to say that they were "not smart enough" or "not good enough."

Carol Gilligan (1982) and her colleagues (Brown and Gilligan 1992) detailed the phenomenon: girls at nine and ten are feisty, filled with spirit and confidence, but as puberty hits, they begin to pull within themselves, doubt themselves, swallow their own voices, and doubt their own thoughts. African American girls hold on to their self-esteem but become more pessimistic about both their teachers and school work than other girls. While boys' period of heightened risk may come earlier when they are pressured early to become "big boys," girls' critical turning point is at adolescence, when they become increasingly aware of the culture that surrounds them. They don't like what they see—objectified bodies, abusive partners, employment disparities, and media denigrations. They hear the message that boys are smarter and that girls shouldn't be too smart. As Lyn Brown writes in *Raising Our Voices: The Politics of Girls' Anger* (1999), girls often feel the expectation that they are supposed to be good, perfect girls who have only kind thoughts. Because they are not perfect, they find themselves in crisis. Doubting themselves, they pull inward and experience a free-fall in confidence. Underestimating their abilities, girls in math and science classes hesitate to enter a computer science environment reputed to be dominated by "supersmart," "logical" (read: unemotional), and competitive male students.

The Experience Gap

One of the biggest challenges in middle and high school computer science classes is that many boys enter school with a great deal of formal and informal computing experience. At the heart of this phenomenon is the "magnetic attraction" that motivates many boys to engage in intense self-guided exploration of computing. High schools therefore typically host a subset of students who are already experts who often know more than their teachers. Girls in high school, then, are often sitting shoulder to shoulder in classes with boys who have spent endless hours learning everything they can about computers and who have friends to turn to when they want to learn even more. This experience gap reaches iconic status with the high school students, nearly always male, who opt out of college to go directly into industry and draw hefty salaries. From their perspective, in a field changing so fast, you are outdated if you go to college.

The Hold of the Computer Game

By middle and high school years, many boys have spent endless hours, alone or with their friends, playing games, manipulating the games so that they do what they want them to do, and in some cases delving into the programming behind the games. Many girls are also interested in games but not generally with the same focus. A 1999 Kaiser Family Foundation study entitled *Kids and the Media @ the New Millennium: A Comprehensive National Analysis of Children's Media Use* found significant gender differences in the time children spend with computer games. At all ages from eight up, boys spend at least twice as much time playing computer games than girls, and beyond age fourteen the percentage of boys who play frequently is some 50 percent greater than for girls.

While game playing resonates with different students in multiple ways, boys give various reasons for becoming consumed with computer games during adolescence. Henry, a first-year Carnegie Mellon student we interviewed, got into computers because he had difficulties interacting with people his age:

> I would go to the computer lab and started playing computer games. . . . And this is how I found my social interaction over the computer, so it was a lot more comfortable for me than dealing with people in school. . . . I had difficulty just approaching someone and talking to them. . . . It would be easier for me to talk over a computer.

He feels that women are "just more built for social interaction than a lot of men are." Another student told us how computers "will always give you attention." Randy described himself "before he began to have a life" when he "chose computers because they do exactly what you want them to do." He goes on to explain that computers "never gripe at you about not being nice enough or not being appropriate enough for a situation." He sums it up as, "You can never be socially mistaken with a machine."

Sherry Turkle (1986), a psychologist and sociologist at MIT, offers an explanation for why computers become particularly seductive for boys at the moment of adolescence. In her article "Computational Reticence: Why Women Fear the Intimate Machine," she contends that adolescence is a time of social upheaval when many children build "microworlds" (sports, chess, literature, music, dance, cars, mathematical expertise) that can become "places of escape." Turkle believes that most children "use these havens as safe platforms from which to test the difficult waters of adolescence" and that for some children adolescence is so threatening that the "safe place seems like the only place" (p. 44). This then is fertile soil for the male hacker culture: "It is during adolescence that the 'hacker culture' becomes born in elementary schools and junior high schools as predominately male—because in our society men are more likely than women to master anxieties about people by turning to the world of things and formal systems" (p. 44).

Turkle (1986) speculates that boys, in response to this anxiety, seek to control the world around them. They feel more safety in a rule-based world populated by objects than in a real world populated by human beings who require intimacy. The computer, then, becomes a perfect medium for these needs, for the "computer is a medium that supports a powerful sense of mastery":

> As people develop their mastery of things and their relational skills with people, most strike a balance. They balance the need for mastery of skills and concrete materials with the desire to do things with people where the results are never as clear. For some people, striking this balance becomes a difficult struggle. Relationships with people are always characterized by ambiguity, sexual tension, the possibilities for closeness and dependency. If these are felt too threatening, the world of things and the world of formal systems becomes increasingly seductive. They turn to formal systems in engineering, in chess, in mathematics, in science. They turn to them for their reassurance, for the pleasures of working in a microworld where things are certain, and "things never change unless you want them to." In other words, part of the reason formal systems are appealing is because they provide protective worlds. (p. 42)

Turkle (1984) describes the constraints of computer games as "those imposed by rule systems, not physical realities or moral considerations." In the games "time might go backwards, people may have superhuman powers, everything is possible," but "what is required is consistency" (pp. 79–80). She finds a compelling explanation in the writings of sociologist Nancy Chodorow as to why boys would turn to the world of things and formal systems to master their anxieties: Chodorow (1999), in her book *The Reproduction of Mothering*, explores how boys' gender identity development is linked to their awareness, at around four or five years old, that they are different from the mother, who is typically their primary care giver. They must separate and become autonomous from their mother; they must become nonfemale. In the absence of a strong nurturing male figure, young boys are left in a tumultuous state of trauma and separation. They therefore yearn for rule-based order. According to Chodorow's theory, girls experience no need for separation, and girls' and women's style of relationship is therefore based on intimacy and closeness. Girls' play and comfort are located in relationships, and it then follows that in the computer world many girls are put off by what they see as boys' zealous fascination with objects and machines rather than people.

Seeking Adventure

Henry Jenkins (1998), the director of the Comparative Media Studies program at MIT, sees boys as looking for areas to explore, adventures to have, and risks to take. In his monograph "Complete Freedom of Movement: Video Games as Gendered Play Spaces," Jenkins (1998) suggests that for urban boys who have no backyard or wide-open territory to explore, the computer game becomes a "virtual play space . . . to reach, to explore, manipulate, and interact with a more diverse range of imaginary places than constitute the often drab, predictable, and overly familiar spaces of their everyday lives" (p. 263). Jenkins believes that the match between boys' play styles and typical game design, which is often based on adventures in fantasy worlds, helps explain the games' popularity:

The "adventure island" is the archetypal space of both the boys' books and the boys' games—an isolated world far removed from domestic space or adult supervision, an untamed world for people who refuse to bow before the pressures of the civilizing process, a never-never land where you seek your fortune. The "adventure island," in short, is a world that fully embodies the boy culture and its ethos. (p. 279)

Creating Media That Appeal to Both Boys and Girls

Feminist psychologist Elizabeth Debold (1997), in a speech entitled "Equity in Technology: Creating Media That Appeals to Both Boys and Girls," claims that current designs of computer games appeal overwhelmingly to boys because "men defined the parameters of play here—and what they project onto these undefined, open spaces reflects male fears and anxieties with which boys identify" (p. 27). She believes that the core of men's anxiety is that males do not have "a clear sense of intrinsic maleness" (p. 27).

According to Debold (1997) boys are continuously bombarded with stereotypes of what it means to "be a man." They must be constantly vigilant and steer clear of activities that have girl attributes: "This anxious vigilance makes boys ripe for constant competition to prove their invulnerability and un-femaleness." Thus "boys' curiosity and interest in violent games are a culturally sanctioned way of acting out scenarios in which they attempt to perfect masculine invulnerability" and that "boys' confusion over masculinity leads them into fantasies of competitive domination to prove they are not vulnerable and don't need their mothers' care" (p. 27).

The Game Girl

"An isolated world far removed from domestic space" is certainly not at the top of most girls' play list. Brenda Laurel (1998), a renowned twenty-year veteran of entertainment software and research, undertook an intensive research initiative at Interval Research Corporation to understand why girls are being left out of the rapidly advancing technology industry. Along with a team of researchers, she talked with leading experts, parents, scout leaders, camp counselors, computer game retailers, and arcade managers. The researchers spent thousands of hours interviewing seven- to twelve year old girls and boys in nationwide "friendship pairs." They concluded that an ideal adventure game for girls would feature everyday "real-life" settings as well as new places to explore. It would have a strong story line and leading characters who are everyday people and as real to girls as their best friends. Success in the game would come through development of friendships. Yasmin Kafai (1998), a professor of education at the University of California at Los Angeles, analyzed 32 video games designed by an ethnically diverse group of sixteen fourth-graders. The student group was evenly divided by gender. In her article "Video Game Designs by Girls and Boys: Variability and Consistency of Gender Differences," Kafai explains the differences between the boys' and girls' game design: the adventure game was the most popular game format, more so for the boys than the girls; most of the girls chose familiar places for their games, such as classrooms, ski slopes, or a fair; boys organized their games more around fantasy places, such as imaginary islands and countries. Games programmed by girls had nonviolent feedback to the game player; games programmed by the boys had violent feedback, such as killing the player and terminating the game in case of a wrong answer.

Controversy about what is the best "girls' game" circulates throughout the industry. Articles and interviews about this "pink software" controversy are presented by MIT professors Justine Cassell and Henry Jenkins (1998) in their edited volume *From Barbie to Mortal Kombat: Gender and Computer Games*. Some analysts believe that Barbie Fashion, a big seller, is no worse than boys' "blood and gore" games and that if Barbie involves girls with computing, then Barbie games should be promoted. Others, however, argue that the Barbie games are based on the crudest stereotype of what girls like and that a much wider range of options should be offered for "girls' games."

Focus groups of girls and teachers convened for the AAUW *Tech-Savvy* report found that girls want to make things rather than destroy things. The violence of boys' games is pointless and boring for them. Girls are interested in games with engaging characters, opportunities for communication and collaboration, a rich narrative, and roles involving positive social action. They relish opportunities to design and create. Although Where in the World Is Carmen Sandiego? has tremendous appeal for both boys and girls, to date, girls still are not playing computer games to the extent that boys are.

Unequal School Resources Compound Home Inequities

Because home and media influences constrict boys' and girls' options and interests, school is needed as a place where options expand and where conditions are equitable. Yet this is not happening. By middle school and high school, boys are more familiar, experienced, and comfortable with computers than most girls. In the computer science classroom, they have found their niche. Girls, the other half of the school population, are not learning computer science in equal numbers. Schools have not figured out how to narrow this gender gap.

The education community has debated the whens, wheres, and whys of using computer technology. And the two of us certainly are not of one mind on this matter. We do feel strongly, however, that girls and minorities need equal access to computers and that diverse participation in the design of technology is critically important for the health of our society. We concur with Kathleen Bennett, the founder of the Girls School for Technology, when in a *Wired News* article, "Girls school seeks to overcome tech gender gap," she says: "It's not that I am trying to turn out little girly geeks. I am trying to ensure that girls who are interested in technical stuff, they get a chance to do it" (Lehmann-Haupt 1997, n.p.).

According to a 1997 Educational Testing Service report, *Computers and Classrooms: The Status of Technology in U.S. Schools,* access to computers, types of available resources, levels of teacher training, and curriculum offerings vary dramatically from school to school. Students attending poor and high-minority schools have less access to most types of technology than students attending other schools. The student-to-computer ratio ranges dramatically from nine to one in Florida to about sixty-three to one in Louisiana.

Girls *are* signing up for classes, such as math or biology, where computing may be involved. Data from a national survey of more than 4,000 teachers in over 1,100 schools across the United States, *Teachers, Learning and Computing: 1998 National Survey,* showed that one out of six science teachers, one out of eight social studies teachers, and one out of nine math teachers said students used computers weekly during their class (Anderson and Ronnkvist, 1999). There was a strong relationship between number of classroom computers and frequency of computer use during class time. The 1998 *National Survey of Information Technology in Teacher Education* (International Society for Technology in Education, 1999) asked public schools to categorize their teachers according to technology-use skill level. The largest percentage of public schools (42 percent) reported that the majority of their teachers (40 percent or more) could be identified at the intermediate level (use of various applications). Nearly as many public schools (38 percent) characterized the majority of their teachers as beginners (learning basics). Only 7 percent of public schools said that the majority of their teachers were at an advanced skill level (use technology in the curriculum), and even fewer (1 percent) public schools placed the majority of their teachers at the innovator or instructor (leads others) level.

Clearly, the students who are interested in learning more about computing but who lack parental instruction, resources at home, and a peer computing community are likely to lose the most when school resources are inadequate.

On Her Own

Tanya, who visited Jane at Carnegie Mellon, is one such student. Tanya is a student at a computer science magnet high school in the Midwest. She was a sophomore when she came to Jane's office to talk about majoring in computer science at Carnegie Mellon. She was dressed in goth-nerd attire: black jeans, oversized teeshirt, her shoes chartreuse fuzzy high risers, hair to her waist, blue lipstick outlined in black. She came at her mother's urging.

Tanya is determined to learn computer science but feels that the computer science magnet program has nothing to offer her. The curriculum is behind the times, the equipment is outdated, and "the teachers don't know their stuff." The three computer science teachers are all math teachers who don't know answers to the questions she asks. Tanya feels that in all of these classes, the teachers do not teach. They just give kids code and ask them to find mistakes. The teachers say that the reason they don't have advanced placement courses or teach C++ is a lack of resources.

Tanya does not have a female friend who enjoys computers as much as she does. She says that some ask her to do their home pages, some chat on the Internet, some look up websites, but only a few even search the web. She believes that her female peers lack confidence but that her male peers think they are smart and go after harder things because they think they can succeed. Tanya talks about how the computer guys are obsessed with computers. It is all they talk about and all they do. Although she is repelled by this behavior, it does not diminish her determination to attend Carnegie Mellon.

Tanya traces her interest in computers back to when her family bought a computer and she began to fool around with it. She admits that a good job with a lucrative salary and job security are is a part of her motivation to learn computer programming. She is tired of not having enough money.

Tanya's guidance counselor suggested that she take a course at another high school, but no nearby high school teaches the programming language C++. She would love to take a course at Carnegie Mellon, but her parents don't have the money. She describes them as "computer illiterates" who got their home computer only because her mother's employer purchased one for her mother to work on at home.

It is unclear what will happen to Tanya. Without the active support system of a teacher, classes, friends, or parents to learn from (even though her parents are supporting her in every way they can), it is hard for her to maintain her enthusiasm.

Unlocking the Clubhouse: High School Is Important

Discouraging influences swirl around girls before they reach high school, but our research shows that high school computer science can be critical for introducing girls to computer science. We found that for almost one-third of the women in our study, a high school programming course became the deciding factor in their decision to major in computer science. This was true for only 9 percent of the males. For males, the "turn on" to computing happens much earlier, usually at home and with friends.

Alexandra was a second-year student at Carnegie Mellon when we first interviewed her. Alexandra's parents were both "in the industry," and she was used to computers and was comfortable around them. Yet before high school, Alexandra used them only for typing. At that time, it was her younger brother who was "really into computers." When Alexandra started high school, she had no intention of taking a computer science class, but her junior high typing teacher strongly encouraged her to take programming rather than typing. Alexandra was hesitant because she was afraid to try something new that she wasn't sure she'd be good at. But Alexandra's teacher insisted.

So Alexandra took Basic in ninth grade and loved it. She took programming for all four years of high school and then decided to major in computer science at college. Alexandra applied and was admitted to Carnegie Mellon. She was a top student all the way through college and is working at a software design firm. Unfortunately, as we have shown, many girls do not have as much success in their high school computer science classes.

As in Alexandra's case above, teachers are critically important for identifying and recruiting girls who would be interested and successful in computer science. But too many teachers and counselors look primarily to boys to have a flair for computing. They are looking for girls who "look like boys"—whose interest in computing mimics boys. But as our research shows, girls' interest in computing is often quite different.

In chapter 3, we turn our attention to the young women who decide to major in computer science in college. We examine their motivations for choosing computing and contrast them with those of a similar group of men. The differences point to a broader vision of what computer science is and who can succeed at it.

Articulating and acting on a broader vision of computing are steps that schools, teachers, and counselors can take to improve recruitment and retention of girls in computing courses. In chapter 7, we discuss a wide range of intervention strategies.

3

Computing With a Purpose

Students' motivation to study computer science varies by gender. For most women students, the technical aspects of computing are interesting, but the study of computer science is made meaningful by its connections to other fields. Men are more likely to view their decision to study computer science as a "no-brainer," an extension of their hobby and lifelong passion for computing.

The women in our study were the survivors of the "boys' club" of high school computing. Some of them self-identified as "girl geeks." We interviewed the former president of her high school's computer club and a student who took pride in being the computer "genius" in her family. Most of these women decided to major in computer science because they did well in a high school class, they found computing came easy to them, and they derived pleasure from it. Almost every woman in our sample is a self-described "math and science person" who enjoys problem solving, doing puzzles, and doing logical thinking tasks. They talk about "the rush in having my program run" and about being at the cutting edge of technology invention. Yet even among these computing-oriented women, we heard about values and preferences that were distinct from those of most male computer science students. This distinction and its ramifications play a key role in the experiences and perceptions of women in computing.

The Decision to Major: The Passionate and the Rational

We have found that women decide to major in computer science based on a broad set of criteria. The simple enjoyment of computing is a leading factor for women, but other factors also weigh heavily in their decisions. They value the versatility of computing, its relation to their interests in math and science, its career path to safe and secure employment, the exciting and changing nature of the field, and the encouragement they received from parents or teachers.

For many male students, in contrast, the decision to major in computer science barely reaches the level of conscious consideration; it is a natural extension of their lifelong passion for computing. Aaron's response to our query about his decision to the major is quite typical: "I don't ever recall really deciding. . . . As long as I've known that there was such a thing as majoring in computer science, I just basically assumed that I was going to be majoring in computer science." When the interviewer asked him if he had ever considered another major, he replied: "Not really." Like Aaron, many of the men in our study are convinced of a perfect fit, while more women describe their decision to major in computer science as "checking it out."

The differences between the choices made by men and women emerge strikingly from our tabulation of their reasons for majoring in computer science, shown in figures 3.1 and 3.2. These graphs tabulate the percentage

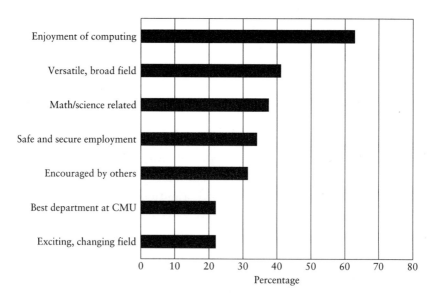

Figure 3.1
Factors in women's decision to major ($n = 32$)

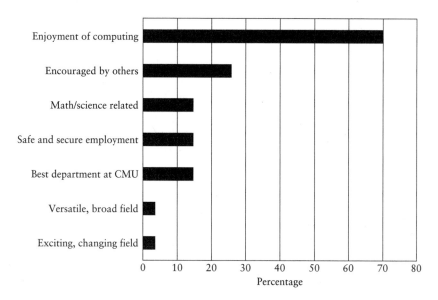

Figure 3.2
Factors in men's decision to major ($n = 27$)

of each group who mentioned the associated factor as a motivation in their decision. Most women take a large number of factors into account: five of the seven categories we tabulated were mentioned by at least 30 percent of the women. In contrast, the only motivation listed by at least 30 percent of the men (in fact, by 70 percent) is the enjoyment of computing.

Versatility of the Field

The versatility of computing is a big draw for women students. As Katina says, "You can do anything with a computer science degree," and "almost any field is computer-related now." She wants to learn skills that will help her get a job and pay back some of her college loans. Then if she likes computers, she can stay with them. Contrasting her job possibilities in biology with those in computers, she calculates:

There is not very much money in biology on the undergraduate level. If you ever want to go to grad school, you could get somewhere from there possibly. But computers are so versatile that basically you could do anything with a computer science degree.

Another Carnegie Mellon student, Andrea, worked with Intel computers in high school. She enjoyed that experience and "caught on very quickly to what was going on." But what really influenced her decision to major was "thinking of the future and what I wanted to do, and it seems that computers are one of the most influential pieces of technology in our world at this time . . . And I thought that if I get into computers, then I'll definitely get a job." Andrea is not exactly sure what she wants to do when she gets out of college. Her heart is in film, but she knows that it is a risky business and wants something enjoyable to "fall back on." She figures that she "can use computer graphics and incorporate that in my film production."

Computing with a Purpose

Besides having a broader set of criteria for majoring in computer science, many women have interests in computing that go beyond the technical aspects. Connecting computing to other fields and working within its human and social contexts make the study of computer science compelling and meaningful for them. For instance, Deborah wants to use computing to study diseases, to "solve the problems of science":

I think with all this newest technology there is so much we can do with it to connect it with the science field, and that [studying diseases] is kind of what I want to do . . . —use all this technology and use it to solve the problems of science we have, the mysteries.

Laurette is interested in the links between computing and "the most efficient way" to use computers in education. Phyllis, a first-year woman student, describes a difference between herself and most of the male students. She says her male peers are focused on "building bigger and bigger computers." "That's fine," she says, "and I'd like to be involved with that, too, but in the long run I want to use computers for what they are now and just use them to help people." She has been inspired by a recent Carnegie Mellon lecture about a robot car that promises to save lives by reducing the number of accidents and deaths caused by human error. Phyllis is determined to not let herself get detached from society but instead to connect computer science to real-world problems:

The idea is that you can save lives, and that's not detaching yourself from society. That's actually being a part of it. That's actually helping. Because I have this thing in me that wants to help. I felt the only problem I had in computer science was that

I would be detaching myself from society a lot, that I wouldn't be helping—that there would be people in third world countries that I couldn't do anything about. . . . I would like to find a way that I could help. That's where I would like to go with computer science.

Another first-year student, Louise, describes a difference she felt between herself and her male peers when she saw her peers' nonchalant response to a lecture on ways that computers can be nonproductive in society:

Everyone just said how boring it was: "Who cares that computers did not benefit anyone? We like computers! We love computers! We know computers! And who cares about the rest of the world"

She describes herself, on the other hand, as someone who scrutinizes the worth of each computing project in terms of what it is doing to change and help the world:

And if you're trying to make something that's going to change the world, that's going to help the world, you have to have some sort of concern about what's your long-term goal. Not just to produce Word 8 . . . or Excel . . . whatever. How is this helping? Or is it helping? Go see if that stuff is doing anything.

Jessica, a woman student who has always done well in math and science, feels deeply that computer science must "make a contribution": "just . . . making video games" is not "worth the energy and talent that it takes." She relates her interest in computer science to her concern for her grandmother's medical condition:

I don't think science—just for making video games—is worth the energy and talent that it takes, but I think it's important if it makes a contribution. So part of that would be a contribution in medicine. My Grandma had a pacemaker, a renal dialysis machine. . . . I've seen the contribution in my family in my life. . . . Medicine has always fascinated me, so I just always wanted to apply my sciences there. And I see the opportunities now, with the computer technology to apply there and that's what I want to do.

Forty-four percent of the women we interviewed and nine percent of the men link their interest in computing to other arenas. We refer to this orientation as "computing with a purpose." This is not to say that the men lack interests outside computing. Sam, for instance, is interested in music and computing. But when he describes his interest in computing, he says "it is the code itself that is interesting, even more so than the actual effect it has." He compares music to programming this way:

Music as an art form is similar to programming as an art form; it's something you can sit down and within a day you can be doing something which has an essence of beauty to it. . . . That process I still find very interesting—how to say what you want to say—so that the code in itself is what is interesting, even more so than the actual effect that it has.

Christopher, a first-year student, relates his attraction to computing to his feeling that "when you write a program, you don't have to worry too much about outside factors influencing how your program is going to run." He contrasts computing to physics experiments, where in physics "you have to take into account gravity and air friction and all these things." For Christopher, computing is "an environment where you can do what you want to do, and you have more control over how you're going to do it." Furthermore, Christopher notes with delight that "you get to do cool things and play around with it and it's fun."

Women's Counternarratives

Women students' descriptions of why they are majoring in computer science are a "counternarrative" to the stereotype of computer scientists who are narrowly focused on their machines and are hacking for hacking's sake. Instead, these women tell us about their multiple interests and their desire to link computer science to social concerns and caring for people. These women may or may not qualify as "people people" on a psychological inventory exam to the same degree as those involved in nursing, social work, or child care, but they need their computing to be useful for society.

Our finding that women students bring contextual concerns to the study of computer science resonates with what feminist psychologists write about women's development. Jean Baker Miller (1976), in her landmark study of women's psychology, *Toward a New Psychology of Women,* writes:

It is true that women, like everyone, are motivated out of the well-springs of their own being. In that sense, we all, at bottom, act on what is moving us individually. It is also true, however, that women feel compelled to find a way to translate their own motivations into a means of serving others and work at this all their lives. If they can keep finding ways to do this, they are often comfortable and satisfied— and they do thereby serve others. This translation of motivation accomplishes an integration that is significantly different from the integration that society encourages in men. In fact, our society specifically discourages men from even attempting anything like this. (p. 63)

Our findings also align with much research on gender and math and science that has found women students bringing contextual concerns to their study. A metaanalysis of research on gender and science by Marcia Linn and Janet Hyde (1989) concluded that a major sex difference in interests in math and science is its perceived usefulness. Schofield's (1995) ethnographic study of the introduction of computers into a high school found that a number of male teachers reported doing things such as building computers for fun or deciding to teach computer science out of a fascination with the subject that led them to switch fields. Not a single female teacher, on the other hand, was fascinated with the computer in this same way. Rather, the female teachers who responded positively to them "tended to speak about their actual or potential usefulness" (p. 161). University of Michigan researcher Jacquelynne Eccles (1994) reports that the Michigan Study of Adolescent Life Transitions, a longitudinal study of approximately 1,000 adolescents from southeastern Michigan, found that "women select the occupation that best fits their hierarchy of occupationally relevant values" and that helping others and doing something worthwhile for society is high in that hierarchy (Eccles, 1994, 600).

Researchers Honey et al. (1991) at the Bank Street College Center for Children and Technology asked twenty-four adult technology experts and eighty early adolescents, approximately equally divided by gender, to describe a science fiction story they would like to write about a perfect computer. They found that the women experts designed their machines to be people connectors, for communication and collaboration. They placed the technology in the context of human relationships. The men experts, in contrast, envisioned technology as "extensions of their power over the physical universe. Their fantasies were often about absolute control, tremendous speed, and unlimited knowledge" (p. 3).

The girls designed household helpers, machines that offered companionship, or devices that they could use to broaden their social and personal networks. The boys, on the other hand, fantasized about extensions of power, often imagining technology that could overpower natural constraints. Besides noting women's concern with relationships and men's concern with power, Cornelia Brunner (1997), a member of the research team and a longtime investigator of the relationship of gender and technology, observed that "The feminine take on technology looks right through the machine to its social function, while the masculine view is more likely to be focused on the machine itself" (p. 55).

Which Orientation Does the Curriculum Support?

In most computer science programs, the early semesters are narrowly focused on the technical aspects of programming, and applications and multidisciplinary projects are deferred to the end. This, unfortunately, gives beginning students, male and female, the false message that computer science is only "programming, programming, programming" and removed from real-world context and concerns. In this context, writes the American Association of University Women Technology Commission (2000), the "cultural emphasis on technical capacity, speed, and efficiency" dominates the scene, and this culture "estranges a broad array of learners," especially women (p. 7). Traditional computer science curriculum and programming assignments often lack the larger interdisciplinary framework that women find important.

Feminist educator Sue Rosser (1990) argues that "insuring science and technology are considered in their social context with assessment of their benefits for the environment and human beings may be the most important change that can be made in science teaching for all people, both male and female" (p. 72). Computer science professor Dianne Martin (1992), in her article "In Search of Gender-Free Paradigms for Computer Science Education," speculates that an integrated approach to computer science would attract more female students. She suggests that "greater attention to values, human issues, and social impact as well as to the mathematical and theoretical foundations of computer science" would redress the balance (p. 1).

Computer scientist Frances Grundy (1998), in her article "Mathematics and Computing: A Help or Hindrance for Women?," explores what lies behind the traditional orientation of computer science. She argues that "pure" computing (such as analysis of algorithms and complexity theory) has historically been considered more prestigious than applied computing because male theoreticians, who are the "inner circle" of computer science, define what is "real computer science." She believes that while "in fact, everything done on a computer requires some abstraction . . . abstraction by itself is not enough; we must be able to set the results of our task back into the real world" (p. 5). Since the majority male "insider" group finds particular value in abstraction and in the joy of playing at the computer, these become dominant parts of the computing curriculum and culture. Thus, many women are left questioning whether computer science has a place for them and whether their orientation will allow for success and a sense of belonging in the discipline.

A Broader View of Programming

Building on the joys that women find in computing is an important task for narrowing the gender gap in the field. Historically, computer science has been associated with number-crunching and quantitative skills to the neglect of more varied thinking and creative activities. In their article "Mismeasuring Women: A Critique of Research on Computer Ability and Avoidance," authors Pamela Kramer and Sheila Lehman (1990) argue that much of the research on the gender gap in computing has mimicked the research on women and math (since computers have been linked to math). In doing so, this research has neglected to look at the larger educational context of how computers are used and how computer learning is different from math learning:

As the use of computers expands in educational and workplace settings, the contexts and applications of their use are rapidly changing so that the presumed closeness of the domains of computing and mathematics knowledge constitutes an increasingly inaccurate portrayal of what experienced and highly skilled computer users describe as being the most advanced types and forms of creative computer-related work. (p. 170)

They argue that, instead, "creative computing now relies at least as much upon language, visual design, problem definition, and organizational skills as upon quantitative analysis" (p. 171).

We, too, found that both women and men find pleasure in areas beyond the traditional quantitative programming lexicon. Here are some of the women's answers to our question "What do you enjoy about programming?"

It seems like solving a giant puzzle. It feels like someone's giving you a Rubik's cube and you have to figure it out. It's something you can think about, play with, and do weird things that no one ever thought of. . . . It's still a challenge that is not in another field that I've found, with possibly the exception of genetics, which is also like a puzzle.

It gives me such a great feeling to have my own little creation. That's the thing about CS that I do really enjoy. It's kind of like an art in itself . . . like it's an art of thinking. And everyone has their own little way of doing an algorithm or something. So that's what I enjoy.

I just like being interactive with a computer. You're almost playing with the computer and making it do things. You can actually see progress before your eyes . . . when you get it to work. . . . It's interaction.

And then at some point I found myself just enjoying the feeling of getting something to work . . . of communicating with this machine and taking my thought, which was not necessarily organized, and turning it into . . . an abstract, organized mathematical language that something as stupid as a machine could understand.

It's kind of like you're given a problem and you have to sit down and solve it. That's your mission, and you do it, and it works, and when it works it's the most amazing feeling in the world!

In a similar vein, here are some answers from men:

Programming? There's that really good sense of accomplishment, the most positive feeling you get when it works. When your program finally works, and you throw your hands up in the air and say, "YES, IT WORKS!" And I just really enjoy problem solving in general and the sort of logical approach to it and the way of thinking that's behind programming.

The part I enjoy about computer science is building things and watching them run. . . . It's just such a great feeling to have created something. . . . In computer science I get a very complete feeling about the wonder of something I've created out of thin air. All my ideas are put together into one thing.

Whether or not people think so, I think that programming is a way of expressing yourself. . . . It's not just a tool. . . . A person that's knowledgeable in computers can do a lot more with computers than you would normally think is possible.

Love of puzzles, creating something from nothing, the art of thinking, interaction, communication: all are facets of the computing endeavor but not always part of the traditional lexicon.

A tally of the factors that students like about programming (table 3.1) shows a few quantitative differences between women and men. Women are more likely than men to cite the satisfaction of getting their program to work, the problem-solving aspects of programming, and the challenge. Despite Kramer and Lehman's (1990) critique, many also report their enjoyment of programming involves its mathematical aspects. The area that men cite significantly more often than women is the creativity of the process. It is not clear to us whether this reflects an independent gender difference, is linked to a primarily male sense of play, or is an effect of the men's overall greater experience. A larger sample of women exhibiting

Table 3.1
Attractions of programming

	Men (n = 35)	Women (n = 37)
Satisfaction in success	40%	57%
Creativity	34	20
Control	31	26
Problem solving	20	49
Challenge	9	43
Ownership	9	14
Logic	9	14
Math related	6	29

substantial experience or a play orientation toward computing would be needed to draw a conclusion.

Programming is fundamental to computer science. Listening to students explain what they enjoy about programming raises the possibility of a wider range of approaches than are currently used to explain programming. It could be that a more expansive set of metaphors could help to refute the stereotype of programming as a dry, mathematical endeavor and engage the interest of a wider range of students.

Summary

IBM (2000) ran a series of magazine advertisements in an effort to recruit a more diverse workforce. One advertisement describes the job held by Grace Liu, educational strategist: "Work with schools to develop and implement tech-based solutions that improve the way students learn." Her experience is listed as "Currently helping San Francisco's school district design a case management tool that prevents students in need from getting lost in the shuffle." This ad stands in sharp contrast to more common computer-related ads that feature young white males in a state of game bliss, focused only on what is on the screen.

Can a creative person, a "people person," care about the world and people and be happy in computer science? While the stereotype says no, a broader vision of what the field is and how it is best taught answers in the affirmative. Computing can be taught in an interdisciplinary setting, honoring the goal of "solving the world's problems." Furthermore, this does not require devaluing the single-minded pursuit of technical virtuosity that marks some of the best computer science students. Instead, it establishes multiple standards of excellence, which together can yield a stronger community of computing professionals than any one by itself. The perspective that computer science can make itself stronger by incorporating the values typical of women in the field changes the question from "How can women change to fit into computer science?" to "How can computer science change to attract more women?"

4
Geek Mythology

What happens when women major in computer science in college? The site of our investigation was Carnegie Mellon University—highly regarded nationally, and regularly ranked among the top three CS programs in the country. When we began our study in 1995, the undergraduate program at the School of Computer Science was overwhelmingly male and included few non-Asian ethnic minorities. Furthermore, the proportion of women leaving the major before graduation was more than double that of men.

These students had entered the program enthusiastic about becoming computer scientists. What happened, and how do their experiences reflect what is happening nationwide? This chapter shows how the male norms of who can do computer science exert their influence at many points throughout a student's college career. Curriculum, culture, peer relations, and faculty expectations reflect the traditional male claim on computing.

The Place: The Carnegie Mellon School of Computer Science

Carnegie Mellon's School of Computer Science is perennially ranked among the top in the nation for both research and education. The school was founded as a department in 1965, was one of the first computer science programs to be created, and has been the source of seminal advances in artificial intelligence, computer design, robotics, and many other areas. Beside the Department of Computer Science, the School includes institutes devoted to research and graduate education in robotics, language technologies, human-computer interaction, entertainment technologies, machine learning, software engineering and other facets of computing.

The future is in the air at Carnegie Mellon, though not in a sleek Silicon Valley way or in an ivy-walled way. The university started out as a technical school, and its industrial roots and Pittsburgh's industrial heritage have left it with a blue-collar feel and ethos despite its high-tech achievements. Although the campus is small and quiet, it is a place for students who want to design and create the technology that is changing the world.

A random walk through the halls of the School of Computer Science leads to encounters with a roving joke-telling robot, a team of robotic dogs that play soccer, and students sporting small, application-specific wearable computers. Student course projects include the construction of elaborate virtual worlds, complex software prototypes developed for industrial "clients," animated computer graphics, and robots that recognize their surroundings and perform useful tasks. Faculty and students alike have spawned dozens of startup companies and have had a large impact on the Pittsburgh and national scenes.

Yahoo! Internet Life recently named Carnegie Mellon the "Most Wired University," and the School of Computer Science yields to none in living up to the title. Newell, Simon, and Wean Halls, the distributed home of the computer science department, are not just wired for computers and printers. Students have taken matters into their own hands over the years, and at various times the status of the Coke and candy machines has been available on the network. A digital camera transmits pictures of the coffee pot in the main lounge over the web. Students subscribe to Zephyr, an early and powerful version of instant messaging that lets them get instant answers to technical questions or receive a news flash when faculty luncheon leftovers are available in the lounge. Beyond the physical wiring of the network (which includes a high-speed wireless network that allows students to remain virtually plugged in while roaming the campus), the School is deeply wired into the nation's technocracy. Flyers posted by the elevator announce talks on current topics by famous computer scientists and business leaders. A former dean co-chaired Bill Clinton's Presidential Information Technology Advisory Committee. Recruiters from hundreds of employers, ranging from Microsoft to tiny startups, stream through in hopes of luring one of the 130 bachelor of science graduates each year.

"You're the Top"

Students entering Carnegie Mellon apply directly to the individual schools, such as the College of Fine Arts, the College of Humanities and Social Sciences, or the School of Computer Science. Admission to the

School of Computer Science is the most competitive. In recent years, fewer than 20 percent of applicants for admission have been accepted (13 percent were accepted for fall 2000).

The first-year academic advisor tells students to "congratulate yourselves for making it here—you are special, in an elite competitive program." He gives them wise advise to "leave your ego and your pride and prejudice at the door" because "you're used to riding on top—now everyone is as smart or experienced as you or more so. . . . Send your egos home. Most of you do not know how to ask for help because you haven't had to before." In the class of 1997, the mean math SAT score was 765; 28 percent had a perfect math SAT score of 800; nineteen students were high school valedictorians; forty students were in the top five of their class.

The school's prestigious reputation is not lost on the students who are admitted. If you are interested in computer science, Carnegie Mellon is "where it is at" says Natalie, a first-year student, who talks about her excitement at being here:

It's like you're at the top of what's happening. You're at the cream of everything. That's so amazing. And in the future, when I get to actually take the courses related to the work that's being done, that's going to be just incredible!

A first-year student says, "CMU embodies computers. If you ever read stuff about computers, you often hear about Carnegie Mellon." Another student told us, "During the summer of my junior year, I'd been reading a bunch of nonfiction books about computers and computer engineering and all this stuff. And there were always three schools that came up there: MIT, Stanford, and CMU." Julie, a sophomore, describes the thrill of being admitted to Carnegie Mellon as "being on top of the world . . . one of my biggest achievements in my life." And then she adds: "I have a lot of achievements, but this was one of the better ones, and they can't take that away from me no matter what they do. I'm going to stick here whether they like it or not."

In 1995, the first year of our study, only seven (7 percent) of the first-year class were women, and female enrollment had hovered at that level for several years. Like other leading computer science institutions, the number of women faculty members stood steady at only 10 percent. Demographically, most of the students were (and are) white or Asian, with very few African American or Hispanic students applying or attending.

Initiation Rites

Students are initiated into the school's culture soon after they arrive at Carnegie Mellon. An introductory computer science lecture can be playful, mischievous, and irreverent. At a raucous introductory lecture for new undergraduates, students hoot and holler as one instructor teases another about playing computer games until two in the morning. During another lecture, students hack into the professor's computer, change the wallpaper of his computer screen, and send him messages. The good-humored professor, who loves a good hack himself, helps fuel the challenge. A student tells us: "I've heard the teacher say, 'I dare you to do [such and such] on the computer.' Eventually somebody does."

Students laugh with glee as the professor in a lecture of computer animation shows, over and over, a simulated car crash that flings an animated driver from a car. This is a world in which humor seemingly mirrors adolescent male sensibilities. In a second demonstration, to illustrate computer-simulated physics, an animated horse tries to leap over a gap and falls short. Down it goes. Students clamor for an encore: "Show us the horse, show us the horse!"

In a presentation to first-year students, a well-known robotics faculty member jokes and tantalizes the students with the tremendous financial potential of the field. Carnegie Mellon students' advantage on the job market becomes part of the banter and humor of the department. Pointing to a slide of four students who worked on one of his projects, he says: "This guy dropped out of school after his second year and started working on this project; this woman retired after five years at the age of 32." He tells the students how he always has his eyes open for the "talent" in the department and calls for the "smartest" students to work on his projects. He appeals to the sense of adventure and risk taking now so valued in this technology-driven world. He gives examples of students going to Antarctica to test a driverless robot and of others entering a volcano. His message is that robotics is a field where the young, adventurous, smart, and energetic can get rich quick.

For students right out of high school, the first year at Carnegie Mellon can be a heady and tension-filled experience. During a presentation about computational biology, a researcher explains that his research team first used Macintoshes and then decided to use "real computers." Laughter and several male fists rise up in the air. Such "in-house" distinctions are argued all the time: "Real" programmers use C; command-line interfaces are better than GUIs; "Macs are for wimps." A professor teaching a programming course in C++ derides the "stupid languages," such as Java, taught in other sections of the course. He calls Java a "programming language for bozos."

A Good Fit

When we asked students, during their first interview, to describe their computer science peers, both men and women responded with the same image. They described a person in love with computers, myopically focused on them to the neglect of all else, living and breathing the world of computing, "at the computer 24/7." Computer science students are said to emerge from being at their keyboards, just once in a while, with a "monitor tan." A campus electronic bulletin board ran a thread about the types of students in the different schools at Carnegie Mellon. The School of Computer Science (SCS) was pegged with descriptive acronyms such as "See, Can't Socialize," "Sleep, Code, Sleep," and "Socially Challenged Students."

For some students, the image of a computer science major as someone who is myopically obsessed with computers is a perfect fit. Ben, a first-year student, is elated at finally finding "all these people who love computers as much as I do." Now he can now talk about "this stuff" without being thought strange:

I like that I can talk and discuss some interesting things that I see with computers and what we can do with them. I mean, that's probably the difference between computer science people and others—that I can actually talk what I want to do. . . . You're so amazed that hey, there's all these other people all of a sudden that love these computers! And I can now talk about this, instead of just talking about just more socially interesting subjects.

Another first-year student, Steven, draws a distinction between *real* computer science students and others:

I think there's two types of people in computer science: there are those who are very smart and work hard, but it's not their life, and then there's me, who could be on the computer all the time. I can go to computer science and spend many, many hours every day. If I had my druthers, I'd spend all day on the computer. I really like summertime because I get to work and I work at a computer all day. I produce programs and what not, and it's like a really good time for me.

This persistent image of the computer science student has deep historical and cultural roots. These roots go back to the days of the early hackers who were discovering the magic of computers at places like Harvard, MIT, Stanford, and Carnegie Mellon. Steven Levy's (1984) book *Hackers: Heroes of the Computer Revolution* describes the lifestyle, passions, and beliefs of these "founding fathers." Hacking was a holy calling, a mission for these young men; computers were considered the magical key to the future. All that mattered about people was their "hacking ability." Brain power was focused on finding the perfect algorithm, and the emotional realm of life was rarely explored. Levy (1984) describes the hacker's world as one without women, in which women and relationships were often regarded as a distraction that took up precious "memory space":

You would hack and you would live by the Hacker Ethic, and you knew that horribly inefficient and wasteful things like women burned too many cycles, occupied too much memory space. "Women, even today, are considered grossly unpredictable," one PDP-6 hacker noted, almost two decades later. "How can a hacker tolerate such an imperfect being?" (p. 83)

Machines, gadgets, and computing power were objects of fascination. Young males would live and breathe computers, with the computer labs becoming their habitats. The notorious description of the early hackers by prominent MIT computer scientist Joseph Weizenbaum, quoted by Levy, still strikes a familiar chord as the expected image of a computer science "geek":

Bright young men of disheveled appearance, often with sunken glowing eyes, can be seen sitting at computer consoles, their arms tensed and waiting to fire their fingers, already posed to strike, at the buttons and keys on which their attention seems to be riveted as a gambler's on the rolling dice. When not so transfixed, they often sit at tables strewn with computer printouts over which they pore like possessed students of a cabalistic text. They work until they nearly drop, twenty, thirty hours at a time. Their food, if they arrange it, is brought to them: coffee, Cokes, sandwiches. If possible, they sleep on cots near the printouts. Their rumpled clothes, their unwashed and unshaven faces, and their uncombed hair all testify that they are oblivious to their bodies and to the world in which they move. These are computer bums, compulsive programmers. (pp. 133–134)

Popular portrayals of computer science students today still play with this image. Doonesbury cartoons feature computer science students oblivious to the world around them; a cartoon about Internet Barbie depicts her sitting in front of her computer wearing sweats and drinking coffee. *The New Hacker's Dictionary* (Raymond 1996) describes the computer geek as "withdrawn, relationally incompetent, sexually frustrated and desperately unhappy when not submerged in his or her craft" (p. 529). While the dictionary's editor believes the stereotype is less true than mainstream folklore would have it, he does describe hackers as having "relatively little ability to identify emotionally with other people" (p. 528) because they are accustomed to spending hours and hours at the computer keyboard.

The Glamorous Geek

Recently, cyberspace money and fame have added a touch of glamour to the nerdy geek image. In this cultural shift, the socially clueless computer nerd has merged with the hip, successful, cool guy. A *New York Times* op-ed piece by Michiko Kakutani (2000) on cyberculture and language opens with the observation that "the lowly geek has become a cultural icon, studied by the fashionistas of Seventh Avenue and the Nasdaq watchers of Wall Street alike" (p. B1). But while computer whizzes may be cooler and more glamorous than before, the expectation is still that young men, sequestered in their cubicles, living and breathing computers, are creating the new world. And the lifestyle of today's computer startups reflects this: offices in Silicon Valley are equipped with bunk beds, workout equipment, and direct lines to the best take-out restaurants. Life is online. Kakutani describes the new language of cyberspace as conjuring up "a chilly, utilitarian world in which people are equated with machines and social Darwinism rules" (p. B1). For example, to be fired or dismissed is to be "uninstalled." A new employee who fits in without any additional training is a "plug and play." Indulging in "nonlinear behavior" means acting irrationally. "Bandwidth" refers to talent or brains, and "client/server action" refers to sex.

Geek Mythology

While both male and female students provide similar descriptions of the typical computer science student, a larger number of students than we had expected (both male and female) say this image of the computer science student "is not me." Contrary to the stereotype, about half of the computer science students we interviewed enjoy computing but also have broad interests and are not glued to their computers. We call this the "geek mythology" paradox: 69 percent of the female computer science majors we interviewed, as well as 32 percent of the men, perceive themselves as different from the majority of their peers and assert that their lives do not revolve around computers.

Robert, a first-year student, does not feel like the stereotypical computer science student. He talks of walking down his dorm hallway and seeing his peers riveted in front of their computers morning, noon, and night:

Every single time I pass by their room they're always on the computer typing away. I don't know what they're doing. Either playing games or they're doing e-mail or whatever. But my roommate, for example, stays up until four in the morning just typing away, and I have no idea what he's typing. But he's just there right in front of the computer in the dark and just typing, typing.

Robert does not spend his life at the computer and complains that this singular focus on the computer flares up wherever computer science students congregate. He cites his experiences in the computer science lounge, where "every time I walk in there, the ongoing conversation is about computers." He adds: "They can't stop talking about computers!" Even the whiteboard is covered in "computer language." Matt, another first-year student, specifically distances himself from the hacker mentality: hackers' "intellectual interests aren't necessarily very broad."

Sarah, a first-year student, complains animatedly about what happens when she goes out for dinner with the computer science crowd. While she tries to move the conversation to other topics, it always lands and seems to stay on computers:

So we're all working on a project, and someone says, "Do you want to go out to dinner?" So six or seven of us pile in a car and go to Eat-N-Park or whatever. And all that happens at the table is I'm sitting there like, "So did any of you hear the new CD by [this band]?" or something, or, "You wouldn't believe this poem we read in my class today!" And they're like, "Oh, we don't care. So anyway, you should see this system that Derrick got. Oh my God! It's so huge! He got an Indy! He got an Indy, and it's like sitting right on his desk just to flaunt at all of us that he's got a better computer than us!" And they're like, "What's the processor speed?" "I don't know, it's somewhere around 100 megahertz!" "Oh!!!" "He's got a 2 gig hard drive!"

Sarah exclaims, "I'm like, 'I don't care! Can't you people talk about anything but computers?' And the thing is, some people here are so happy for the fact that they finally have these friends that just talk about computers! It's like, 'Hey, we can go out to dinner and talk about computers, and people won't laugh at us anymore because computers are hip!'"

Geek Myth More Damaging to Women

While the stereotype of the computer science student as someone who is myopically focused on computing is rejected by many male and female students, women report more distress and are more affected by the perceived difference between themselves and their peers. One-third of the male students we've interviewed say they differ from the stereotype, that they have a broader range of interests than just computing. But twice as many women (more than two-thirds of those we interviewed) feel different from the stereotype. And 20 percent of the women we interviewed question whether they belong in computer science because they feel they do not share the same intensity in focus and interest that they see in their male peers.

Donna is a junior who was very involved in the Internet before coming to Carnegie Mellon. She has always regarded herself as a math-science person. By her second semester, Donna doesn't think that computer science is for her. Comparing her own set of interests to those of her male peers, who seem so driven by computers, she began to doubt her place in the field: "It's not my passion like everyone else. They're all really into it." In her particular case, her boyfriend is "really into robotics" and is planning on going to graduate school and becoming a professor. When we ask her to describe why computer science is not for her, she says:

When I have free time, I don't spend it reading machine learning books or robotics books like these other guys here. It's like, "Oh my gosh, this isn't for me." It's their hobby. They all start reading machine learning books or robotics books or build a little robot or something, and I'm just not like that at all. In my free time I prefer to read a good fiction book or learn how to do photography or something different, whereas that's their hobby, it's their work, it's their one goal. I'm just not like that at all; I don't dream in code like they do.

Comparing herself to peers who "dream in code," who do nothing but computer science, she questions her own motivation and whether she belongs:

Sometimes I feel they [male peers] have a motivation that's deeper than I do. It's weird. I have that kind of feeling like, "What? Do I belong in this major if they love programming that much?" And I have friends who will be like, "Well, I am going to teach myself a new language," and they'll go pull an all-nighter. I don't have that motivation, so am I in the right department? Am I in the right thing?

Each student's self-evaluation becomes a critical part of his or her sense of belonging in computer science, and the myopically obsessed computer whiz types have become the reference group—a frame of reference for each student's self-evaluation and attitude formation. An exceptionally high level of obsession and expertise has become the expected norm and has raised the bar for the level of knowledge, interest, and expertise identified with computer science majors. For women, seeing most of their male peers as totally absorbed in computing, the fear that "I don't seem to *love* it as much as the men, and therefore I don't belong," lurks in many women's doubts.

Can a Computer Science Major Find Balance?

Many of the women we talked with are alienated from and resistant to a culture they find insular, isolating, and "out of balance." "Scary" and "afraid" are words that recur again and again in women's interviews when they describe qualities associated with being a computer science major. Louise, a second-year student, wants to do well in her major and become a good computer scientist. But, she told us, she is unwilling to "sacrifice the rest of my life for computing." Moreover, she believes many male students will make the sacrifice:

I think it's real important to do well in my major and become a good computer scientist, but at the same time I'm not going to sacrifice the rest of my life for it. But I think there are quite a few guys that do. Their whole life is pretty much centered around their classes and programming and programming outside of class, and I just don't think women do that for anything, at least not that I've seen. That's very rare. . . . You see all the guys who are like, "Wow, this is my life." You see their drive. You think you can't compete with this. You can, it's just that some people aren't willing to and become uncomfortable with all that.

So women in computer science find themselves in a perplexing dilemma. Because young males have flocked to computer science and have become compulsively attached to computing, the computing culture reflects their domination and desires and projects the male way as the way to be in computer science. Many women, on the other hand, prefer a life that is *not* singularly focused.

Jennifer, a first-year student, likes computers a lot and knows that this is what she wants to study. But she is dismayed by the fact that she sees very few people in computer science who have balance in their lives and "enjoy other stuff besides computer science." Seeing her peers, sitting in front of computers for hours on end, with no expression on their faces, scares her:

Because I see these people. They can sit in front of a computer for hours and hours, and they would have no expressions on their face, and they would just do whatever. And then it scares me because I don't want to make computers my life. It's part of my life. I know this is what I'm going to do. I like to study, I like computers, but I can't make it my life like some of the other people do. . . . I only know a few people in computer science who seem to enjoy other stuff besides computer science. They seem to have a balance. I admire those people, though.

Another student, Barbara, who is contemplating changing majors, says there is "no specific thing that I dislike about computer science. I guess it's just the general atmosphere." Barbara is afraid of becoming so myopically focused on the computer that her links to other interests will disappear. She says: "I've heard of certain people that just go into writing code, and . . . all their focus is into that, and they kind of ignore everything outside that scope. That's one thing I'm afraid of becoming." Nancy, as well, knows she wants to work with computers but "does not live to program" and values the balance she has in her life. Nancy says she "doesn't hate computer science" but "doesn't like it as a lifestyle":

I don't live to program. I know guys who live to program, or at least they seem to. You find them on the weekends doing nothing but programming and I just think, "How can they do that?" I guess I think I'm more balanced.

The rub for women in computer science is that the dominant computer science culture does not venerate balance or multiple interests. Instead, the singular and obsessive interest in computing that is common among men is assumed to be the road to success in computing. This model shapes the assumptions of who will succeed and who "belongs" in the discipline.

Jacquelynne Eccles (1994) is a researcher from the Institute for Social Research in Ann Arbor, Michigan, who has been studying women's occupational and educational choices for over twenty years. She investigates whether socialization could lead women and men to have different hierarchies of core personal values. A longitudinal study of adolescent life transitions shows that "girls place more value than boys on the importance of making occupational sacrifices for one's family and on the importance of having a job that allows one to help others and do something worthwhile for society" (p. 600). In data collected from gifted female and male subjects, the women rated four areas more highly than did the men: family, friends, richness of one's cultural life, and joy in living. The men rated occupation as having higher importance than did the women.

In related research on female and male interest patterns, girls scored higher than average on several interest clusters; in contrast, boys often evidence a more unidimensional set of interests. Eccles theorizes that women place higher value on having a multifaceted life rather than being solely focused on one dimension. According to Eccles, women calculate "perceived cost" of their occupational choices, influenced by many factors such as anticipated anxiety, fear of failure, fear of social consequences of success, and loss of time and energy for other activities (p. 598).

Women in Computing: Guests in a Male-Hosted World

If the only option for being in computer science is abandoning a balanced life and other interests, many women will find the cost too great. Suzanne is a top second-year student and a keen observer of social relations. She says, "It doesn't help that a lot of the guys seem to just like to sit in front of the computer all the time and just sit . . . play games or write games. . . . If a female doesn't do that, to them it implies that they're not as interested." How can these women cling to balance and compete with men who are so singularly focused on the computer? One student tells us that she wants to be "a very broad person. I mean, that is a part of me just as much as anything else." But then adds, "But I guess if you want to be specialized, you have to focus."

A critical part of attracting more girls and women to computer science is providing multiple ways to "be in" computer science. Concern for people, family, "balance in life," novels, and a good night's sleep should not come at the cost of success in computer science. But the full acceptance of this proposition cuts against the dominant culture of the field.

Carnegie Mellon is certainly not the only computer science department that recognizes that the expectations associated with "being a geek" have become a major deterrent to the recruitment and retention of women students. Ellen Spertus (1993), currently an assistant professor of computer science at Mills College, was an MIT graduate student when she wrote a paper entitled "Why Are There So Few Female Computer Scientists?" She describes the hacker culture as part of the masculine environment and points out a difference in priorities between men and women:

It is important to remember that women who do not throw themselves into the computer world might not be inferior to men, but that sacrificing everything to computers might not be something that a psychologically healthy human being does. Perhaps men and women alike would be better off if some jobs and hacker cultures did not require giving up the rest of their lives. (p. 35)

More recently, MIT launched a recruiting campaign whose message was that being a male geek was not a prerequisite to studying there.

In Europe, too, hackers have been recognized as a negative cultural influence on women in the field. Bente Elkjaer (1992), a Danish researcher, characterizes women's experiences in computer science as being "guests in a male-hosted world." At the Norwegian Institute of Technology, computer science has the lowest percentage of female students (8 percent) of all departments. Instead of focusing solely on "deficiencies" in girls, such as fear of technology and lack of self-confidence, researchers Hapnes and Rasmussen (1991) have examined the culture of computer science. They studied how the minority hacker ("key-presser") culture has come to dominate the field. While many male students and professors share certain values with the hackers, most of the female students distance themselves from a culture that myopically focuses on the computer as machine. These researchers conclude that "the female students distance themselves from the hackers, because the hackers represent what they do not want to be. The female students do not want an intimate relationship with the computer. Intimacy belongs to people, not machines" (p. 399).

Overcoming Geek Mythology

The AAUW's *Tech-Savvy: Educating Girls in the New Computer Age* (2000) describes focus groups with seventy middle school and high school girls and surveys of 892 teachers. The conclusion of these studies is that girls today have a "can do, but don't want to" attitude toward computing (p. 5). The authors argue that while the low number of girls in computer science is often attributed to computer phobia, such behavior is instead "a choice that invites a critique of the computing culture" (p. x). Instead of hearing a lot about computer anxiety, the Commission heard girls critiquing the culture of the field—the way computer science is conceived and taught and the violent way it is used in computer games.

Industry and government are campaigning to change the geek image. IBM has recently run advertisments that profile interesting, well-rounded, socially concerned employees. The government is attempting to burnish the image of programmers and encourage more young people to enter the field. Anticipating a shortage of programmers and software developers, the U.S. Department of Commerce has planned an advertising campaign using celebrities and teenagers themselves to communicate the message that programming is "cool, exciting and you can do it."

A Matter of Expectations

The following e-mail exchange took place between two high school computer science teachers who were part of our summer program on gender equity and computing (see chapter 7). The male teacher initiated the discussion about the small numbers of female students in his computer science classes. He observes that he has "any number of boys who really love computers" and that "several parents have told me that their sons would be on the computer programming all night if they could":

I have yet to run into a girl like that. A couple are Internet nuts, but that's social, not programming. Where are the girls that love to program? My girls sit up and take notice when I talk about programming as a good way to make a living, but look at me funny when I talk about it as fun. The boys think money is nice but fun is where it's at. Why is this?

Instead of responding with a list of reasons why girls are not like the boys, a female computer science high school teacher identifies this teacher's question as the same misassumption made by many of her students: they also look in the wrong places for signs of being interested in computers. They believe that staying up all night programming is a sign of love for computer science and that not doing so is a sign that one doesn't love it. But she disagrees. She talks about taking her first programming course in college and how she "fell in love with it." She said it was "organized, logical, and yes, fun." However, she did not stay up all night doing it. She says she "did not even spend a majority of my time programming" and did not program on her own, coming up with games or entertainment. She said she enjoyed the programming assignments "immensely," enjoyed the challenge, and especially enjoyed the "practical problems." But, she adds, "My point is that staying up all night doing something is a sign of single-mindedness and possibly immaturity as well as love for the subject. The girls may show their love for computers and computer science very differently."

She emphasizes that if we are using a single male model to identify potential computer science students, we will miss many potential female (and male) students:

If you are looking for this type of obsessive behavior, then you are looking for a typically young, male behavior. While some girls will exhibit it, most won't. But it doesn't mean that they don't love computer science!

It is important to note that it is not only women who resist a myopic focus on computers. Some men resist a narrow orientation but do not question their ability to become computer scientists because their gender has not rendered them suspect. The social history and culture of computing, based on the activities and culture of boys and men who have made computing the central focus of their lives, contribute to boys' sense of belonging and girls' sense of "outsidership" in computer science.

The model of a successful computer science student is viewed through a male prism. This perspective bolsters men's confidence and sense of belonging. The same culture expects little success from women. Women's interest in and attachment to computing are considered outside the norm, and their abilities are never taken for granted. This places women students, especially those who resist becoming myopically focused, at high risk in the discipline.

5

Living among the Programming Gods: The Nexus of Confidence and Interest

Several people who heard about our research project felt that there are few women in computer science because "computer science is boring for women." Interest in a subject, though, is influenced by factors beyond an individual's intellectual preference for an abstract body of knowledge. In this chapter, we look at the ways that interest in computing is extinguished in many college women and how their exit statements that they are "just not interested" are a misleading summary of a complex process. Many once-enthusiastic female college students find themselves in a descending spiral of eroding interest through the corrosive effects of lack of confidence, negative comparisons to peers, poor pedagogy, and biased environments.

Lily is a first-year undergraduate computer science major who entered Carnegie Mellon with a great deal of enthusiasm. Her interest was first sparked in high school, when she took an advanced placement computer science course at the suggestion of her guidance counselor. "As soon as I started taking that course in programming, I realized I loved it. . . . I absolutely loved it." Her enjoyment of a summer programming job solidified her decision to major in computer science. She enjoyed "the challenges the programmer faces" and found the problem solving to be "fun." By the end of her second college semester, though, Lily's enthusiasm for computer science plummeted. She says, "In high school, when I'd go home from class, I would be like, 'Oh, let's program a little.' But now I am just like, 'Let's not bother.'" All around her, she experiences her peers (mostly male) as doing much better with much less effort. She talks about her loss of confidence. Since her interest in computing doesn't seem to measure up to the all-consuming love of computing that many of her peers have, she begins to question whether she is really interested in computing after all.

Several semesters later, Lily transfers out of computer science into English. She describes her disappointment in having transferred out. She is not unhappy in English; she loves the humanities. But she remembers how much she loved programming and had wanted to major in computer science and feels dismayed with how her interest has waned. Lily's experience is not unique.

"Everyone Knows So Much More"

Sara, a first-year student, entered Carnegie Mellon excited about majoring in computer science. Sara had been computing since she was young; computing was her hobby. Her family thought of her as the "computer genius." In high school, she loved programming and advanced placement computer science. She thought it was easy and that "computer science people are cool!" At Carnegie Mellon, Sara placed out of the introductory course. With all this, Sara still found it "scary" how much computing her peers already knew. She says, "The problem is the friends that I have in computer science know so much about it—more than is expected."

Sara is right. Students at Carnegie Mellon know a lot about computing. Throughout the campus—from fine arts to engineering—many students are extraordinarily knowledgeable about computing. The history of Carnegie Mellon as one of the birthplaces of modern computing, as well as the computing-related orientation of many of the disciplines, attract students who are intensely interested in and knowledgeable about computing. In a study of the introduction of computing into the academic instruction at Carnegie Mellon during the early to mid-1980s, researchers L. Sproull, S. Kiesler, and D. Zubrow (1987) caught an irony of the place:

CMU clearly values computing quite highly. But in their enthusiasm for computing, its managers and experts have created situations in which it is hard for novices to be enthusiastic. Like the overzealous tour guide who forces his charges to climb endless sets of steps for the perfect view, to eat sheep's eyeballs for the perfect culinary experience, and to sit through a five-hour native poetry reading, this organization can produce more cultural dropouts than recruits. (p. 194)

Scattered throughout the university are students who wanted computer science as their first choice of major but who were not accepted because of the competitive admissions. Every seat in the department is highly coveted.

This leads to campuswide envy (mixed in with some contempt on the part of students who still see computer science majors as asocial geeks) and high expectations of how much a computer science student should know. As a result, the bar of what one should know, if one is a computer science major at Carnegie Mellon, is raised astronomically high. For students, including most women, who have not spent their tender years in front of a computer, these high expectations can be discouraging. This phenomenon is especially difficult for first-year students, who often were at the top of their high school classes and the computer whizzes of their schools or families. Suddenly they are surrounded by new faces, many of who were also at the tops of *their* schools, and they begin to recalibrate themselves in relation to their new classmates.

Carmela, a sophomore who began playing with computers when she was four, started programming when she was five or six, and competed on her high school programming team, tells us how the computing knowledge of her classmates overwhelmed her. Men's comments about how easy assignments were, when she had been working so hard on them, shook her confidence and then diminished her interest in programming:

Then I got here and just felt so incredibly overwhelmed by the other people in the program (mostly guys, yes) that I began to lose interest in coding because really, whenever I sat down to program there would be tons of people around going, "My God, this is so easy. Why have you been working on it for two days, when I finished it in five hours?"

Could this be a case of male boasting? Norma, a first-year student, talks about her assumption that the male students know more. She says that she thinks "it is the way they carry themselves." She has met some guys who "don't know anything" but who appeared at first that they did. She says that she is learning that "if I meet a guy who is a computer science male student, I shouldn't assume that they know everything":

I mean they're obviously here because they're very bright and they think a certain way, but when it comes to programming . . . some of them haven't had the formal training, and that leads me to believe that they just [exude] confidence, I guess. It is not so much of what they know.

While male posturing and boasting may lead women to feel they know little compared to their male peers, most women college students have had less computing experience in high school and, especially, in informal, extracurricular computing activities. Of 136 incoming computer science students surveyed in 1998 to 1999, men averaged 3.24 on a 1 to 5 scale of programming experience level, and women averaged 2.14; 38 percent of women and 7 percent of men ranked themselves as beginners; and 12 percent of women and 45 percent of males ranked themselves at 4 or 5. These self-assessments, which could include some estimation bias, are consistent with the percentages of students who reported having paid professional programming experience: 25 percent of men reported such experience, whereas just 4 percent of women did so. Also, more males start programming early "for fun," pursue it as an interest on their own, and take it further.

Repeatedly in our interviews, male students refer to personal programming projects outside of class or work. Most females, by contrast, gained most of their experience in high school classes and seldom programmed outside of school. Although 38 percent of first-year men in our study report significant out-of-school, self-initiated programming experience before coming to college, just 10 percent of first-year women had similar experiences prior to college.

While men do have more experience, prior computing experience level turns out not to be a predictor of eventual success in the program. Prior computing experience can have a significant impact on confidence and comfort in the program and might give some truth to the impression of many women that "others catch on so much more quickly." It also can lead to grade disparities in early courses. However, self-ratings of programming experience are lower for female persisters than for women who transfer out—3.0 to 3.4, on a 1 to 5 scale with 5 being most experienced (see chapter 6). Still, the experience gap contributes to women's unease with what they don't know.

One student, Jeanne, reports standing next to a male computer science major as both were admiring a black wine bottle. Her conversation partner said, "It looks like a NEXT box." She said, "What's that?" and he said, "I can't believe you are a computer science major and do not know what a NEXT box is." She says, "This is what you get a lot of when you are a computer science major."

Not only do women perceive male students as knowing more computer science, but many experience men as doing it with greater ease and more "naturally." When an interviewer asks Penny, a second-semester student, whether her interest in computer science has increased since being at

Carnegie Mellon, she replies by describing a computer graphics lecture as "the most exciting lecture I have ever attended." But then she adds:

I'm actually kind of discouraged now. Like I said before, there's so many other people who know so much more than me, and they're not even in computer science. I was talking to this one kid, and . . . oh my God! He knew more than I do. It was so . . . humiliating kind of, you know?

Penny says that she doesn't know what she thinks she needs to know and that "inhibits my willingness to continue." She knows that this should propel her drive to learn more, but it doesn't. In addition to being humiliated, she feels "like I'll always be behind, and it's discouraging."

The Erosion of Confidence

Researchers on gender and math and science have found that self-confidence, not ability, is the significant difference between male and female science students. In their seven-university study, E. Seymour and N. Hewitt (1997) observed that most women they encountered had entered college at a peak of self-confidence, based on good high school performances, good SAT scores, and a great deal of encouragement and praise from high school teachers, family, and friends. Then, "within a relatively short time of their entry to college, women who felt intelligent, confident in their abilities and prior performance level, and who took their sense of identity for granted, began to feel isolated, insecure, intimidated, to question whether they belonged in the sciences at all and whether they were good enough to continue" (pp. 255–256). In her article "Math Self-Concept: How College Reinforces the Gender Gap," Linda Sax (1994) analyzed a survey of over 27,000 college freshman students and a follow-up four years later. She found that self-concept declines for both men and women in college math classes but that the "magnitude of the decline is greater in more selective schools" and that "the decline in math self-confidence in selective colleges is more pronounced for women than for men" (p. 149). A student's self-perception is formed by self-assessments of her abilities in comparison with those of her peers.

Women's loss of confidence is especially severe in historically male-dominated fields. According to S. Brainard and L. Carlin's (1997) six-year study of women in science and engineering classes at the University of

Washington, many women suffered a steep drop of confidence following their freshman year and never fully recovered. A study of North Carolina State engineering students found that the women in the first-year cohort began the semester less confident, on average, than the men about their ability to succeed in engineering (Fuller et al., 1997). And even though they performed about the same as the men, with an average GPA of 2.89 compared to 2.83, they lost more confidence in ability than did their male counterparts. Indeed, the difference in the level of confidence between men and women is so pronounced that the men who did not matriculate were significantly more sure of their ability to succeed in engineering than were the women who did matriculate. In a 1988 study of premedical students (Fiorentine, 1988), women rated themselves lower than the men rated themselves on every scale—including overall academic ability, mathematical ability, writing, popularity, and expectations of how well they thought they would perform as a physician. While the attrition rate for the students who received good grades was the same for males and females, the attrition rate among the students who received a poor grade was higher for women.

While women in our study expressed more doubts about their ability than most men, course grades for most computer science classes were comparable between the women and the men students. Average grades for men and women were nearly identical in the first programming course most students take, with most students doing well. And computer science grades for the second year and beyond are fairly similar, with women averaging 2.99, and men, 3.08. The only significant exception has been in the data structures course, typically taken in the second semester, where women did not do as well as men, on average.

Small Injuries Hurt Women More

While the confidence of many women hangs on a razor's edge, our tracking of students has shown that problems with curriculum and teaching hurt all students, but they hurt women and minorities even more. For instance, all students in the Carnegie Mellon program take a data structures course (15–211, Fundamental Structures of Computer Science) during the second or third semester. The preceding introductory courses are small, typically twenty-five students, and the first-year advising staff members are devoted to teaching and make themselves available to students many hours a day. Course 15-211, though, has historically been a large class with a rotating teaching staff. It is a lecture course where computer science majors of all experience levels are students together in a course for the first time. Almost all students complain that this class tries to teach too broad a range of students. Students who are less experienced feel that the professors assume students know more than they do.

In academic year 1997 to 1998, for example, this class became a downhill turning point for many women students. Female students with less experience felt vulnerable in unfamiliar territory. In our sample, women's grades in 211 averaged 2.71, while men's grades averaged 3.21. Women students voiced more criticisms of the teaching, large class size, and assignments and frequently concluded that having trouble in 211 meant that things would get worse in subsequent courses. Many of the women felt lost, unsupported, unconnected, and unable to bolster their own sense of belonging in the field. On top of this, despite a substantial staff of teaching assistants, they felt they had little contact with faculty who could give them much-needed encouragement and support.

While the women report feeling like they were "drowning," most men in our sample describe 211 as "easy," "boring," and "repetitive." This, then, adds an extra layer of discouragement on top of women's frustration. As one woman student said:

It is annoying to pick up a 15–211 assignment (which all my friends say is easy) and spend several hours trying to figure out what to do, then have to constantly get help from a smarter friend because I don't understand it. Then I overhear comments about how easy it was and how this person loved it and did it in four hours or something, and it seems like I can't do anything on my own.

Much prior research shows that female students in technical disciplines, perhaps partly because of their "outsider-ness," are especially vulnerable to poor teaching, inhospitable teaching environments (such as large classes), and unhelpful faculty. Even a small proportion of such occurrences against an otherwise welcoming and supportive background can have severe negative effects. One woman who transferred out discussed how a perception of poor teaching contributed to her leaving computer science:

I get the impression that the computer science department here doesn't actually "teach." They just hand out assignments, and they say, "Do them." And they figure if you can do the assignment, then you know what's going on. I guess they figure if you can handle four years of just doing that constantly, then you're really good at it.

"You Are Here Only Because You Are a Girl"

When we asked a student how she experienced being one of a minority of women, she said: "The guys rub it in. . . . You know, they come in and say, 'Just because you're a girl, you got accepted.'" She goes on: "I guess they're just pulling your leg or something, but it still doesn't feel good when they come back and say things like that." Another woman told us about a male peer who said something like, "Girls . . . they just bring you girls here to make our computer science department look better. . . . They don't really expect you to be able to code, but if you need help, you got the goods to get help from any guy you want." A quarter of the women we interviewed reported hearing comments implying that the only reason they were admitted was because of their gender.

Research from other universities reveals similar environments for women in computer science, in which comments from male peers, seemingly incidental or random, accumulate to make women feel undervalued and ultimately unwelcome. Ellen Spertus's (1991) report on MIT women in computer science, "Why Are There So Few Female Computer Scientists?," concludes that these comments and behaviors are "the symptom of a more fundamental problem: lower expectations for females" (p. 14). Women then internalize these low expectations with the air they breathe.

Virginia Valian (1998), professor of psychology and linguistics at Hunter College, in *Why So Slow? The Advancement of Women*, writes about perceptions of gender differences—gender schemas—and how they accumulate in professional life so that men tend to be overrated and women underrated. She writes that "people's expectations of us lead us to perform in a way that meets those expectations" and that "even when no one is approving or disapproving of us at the moment, our conceptions of ourselves are based in part on a history of other people's views" (p. 145).

When we asked a student in her second interview how it felt being a woman in the program, she said, "It's very disheartening. If you are continually told that you're hopeless, eventually you will start believing it. How long can you put up with that?"

A second-year student, Stephanie, tells us that when a male student said to her "Oh, you only got into computer science because you are a girl," she retorted: "I don't think so! You know, I had higher SATs than you. Shut up!" She tells us that she was "not the only one who got that." One of her friends came to her when she was a first-year student and told Stephanie that that some guy said she got into computer science only because she was a girl. Stephanie said, "It's not true. Just say, 'My SATs were better than yours,' and they'll shut up, even if that's not true." At the end of this story, Stephanie tells us, "I mean, that's one thing you get a lot of."

While most of the women say that all but a few of their male peers are nice and helpful, 22 percent of the women we interviewed mention having heard that they got in only because of their gender, and an additional 11 percent wonder if this may be true. Some women, although a minority, say that they are completely comfortable in the program and that the small number of women is irrelevant to their experiences. Some even enjoy feeling unique and take pride in being one of a special few. Other women struggle with their doubts but emerge stronger, their self-confidence resistant to such concerns. Even a woman student who feels that being a woman has no effect on her, however, reveals the sting of the admission barbs: "You know, I just hope sometimes that I didn't get into computer science because I am a girl. . . . Other than that, it [being a woman] doesn't affect me very much, you know? In fact, I think maybe some people think I am even cooler."

The irony in these accusations is that until recently admissions standards for the computer science program at Carnegie Mellon arguably carried a small bias against women. Men and women were judged by identical numerical formulae, including a heavy reliance on the SAT math score, which many studies have shown to systematically underpredict women's college performance. Although final admissions decisions were subject to human judgment and review, nonetheless women tended to earn slightly higher grades than men once enrolled at the university. In the past few years, the university has adopted a more holistic approach, which we discuss in chapter 8.

"A Threat in the Air"

Professor Claude Steele (1997) of Stanford University studies what happens to minority and women students when they find themselves in academic situations in which negative stereotypes and expectations are active. In his article "A Threat in the Air: How Stereotypes Shape Intellectual Identity and Performance," he argues that stereotypes and low expectations for women in math and science play a major role in women's loss of interest in these fields. In situations in which negative group stereotypes apply, there is a "threat in the air" that leads group members to be fearful of confirming the stereotype. This fear creates "stereotype vulnerability," which can lead to poorer performance and "disidentification" with, or detachment from, the field.

One example of Steele's research on stereotype vulnerability involves giving high-achieving men and women a difficult math test. He has found that when women are told that the test results show a gender difference, their test scores drop. When they are told that there is no gender difference, their test scores rise. His research has been replicated in many different settings and shows how the stereotype that women are less able than men in math negatively affects women's test performance. A similar experiment tested the effect of stereotype threat on African Americans students. When they were given a test, asked to note their race on the test, and told that it would test their analytical ability (which is poor according to the stereotype of blacks), their scores dropped relative to a situation where they were not asked to note their race.

Steele believes that stereotype vulnerability explains the drop of interest and disidentification with a field—especially among woman in male-dominated fields and African Americans in academic settings in general. He concludes that these students disidentify with a field in a "retreat of not caring about the domain in relation to the self. As [disidentification] protects in this way, it can undermine sustained motivation in the domain" (1997, 614). This is one way of understanding the nexus of confidence and interest and provides a deeper understanding of women students' sense of vulnerability and the conclusion of some that "computer science just doesn't interest me."

A Vicious Circle

Julie, a junior at the time, describes how interwoven confidence and interest are for her:

I enjoy computer science, but it's not my life. . . . Part of it is a confidence thing . . . because I sometimes feel like I'm not nearly as good as so many other people. I'm not a whiz. I'm not someone who gets things instantaneously. It just feels like everyone around me does. So when you feel like you are not as good at things, you lose a little bit of interest.

Julie puts her finger on a pattern we hear from many students. The pattern begins when, feeling overwhelmed by coursework and outclassed by peers, a woman begins to doubt her own abilities. At this stage, our interviews often find women expressing doubt about their "fit" in computer science but still feeling keen interest. Eventually, though, if a woman's confidence does not return, a process similar to Steele's concept of disidentification ensues, and her interest also declines.

In the peculiar setting of computer science, this pattern can reinforce itself, in that a lessening of interest can cause a woman to doubt herself even more. If the archetypal computer science student is consumed with passion for the field, the thinking goes, perhaps a student with less interest simply does not belong in computing. Thus women can find themselves in a downward spiral of interest and confidence.

What About the Inexperienced Men?

What about the novice men, those with little precollege computing experience? How do they do in the program? The males with less experience are somewhat more likely to transfer out than those with more experience. Of the five males in our sample who transferred to other departments, four had relatively little programming experience. Of nineteen males with the least experience, four transferred out and four left Carnegie Mellon. Among the four who left the university, three were African American and one was Hispanic. There could not be a clearer signal that the experiences of racial minorities in computer science must be more fully understood and addressed.

Males with the least experience are more likely than other men to voice the concerns women speak of: they express doubts about their ability, and some feel like they don't quite fit and don't know what others are talking about. Even so, the self-doubt is not nearly as intense and consuming as it is for many of the female students. We believe this is because the men's abilities are not continuously under suspicion because of their gender.

While some males' confidence drops, those who face difficulties with coursework do not struggle under the additional burden of the presumption that they are somehow inferior by virtue of their gender. Nor do they have the pressure of feeling they are representative of their gender. To examine this further, we selectively sampled male students with little programming experience. We found that these "novice males" did not express the same level of distress as female peers with similar or even more programming experience. While the absence of these types of feelings in the men's interviews could be due partly to a difference in communication style between men and women, causing men to be less likely to show vulnerability, none of the male students we interviewed mention pointed barbs or snide remarks directed their way. None of the men report having his existence in the department questioned because of his gender. And none reported a fear of being thought of as a "stupid male" if he asked a question in class.

An atmosphere of negative expectations about their gender's abilities places women at double risk in computer science. A female student describes the difference between the women's and men's learning environment this way:

> They [male students] have the pressure to do well, but they don't have excess pressure from us [women] saying, "You know, you're pathetic, you just got in because you're a guy," or something. We don't give them that. . . . Their confidence hasn't hit rock bottom because of that. They tell us all the time, and it isn't something we like to deal with. We shouldn't have to deal with it.

Lori tells us that "there are classes where I am really afraid to speak or to ask a question because I am afraid that it's a stupid question." She feels "if I, as a girl, ask the question, they would always think 'Oh, the stupid girl.'" Therefore, she usually waits after class and talks to the teaching assistant or the lecturer. She adds: "I know that sounds horrible, but I'm really scared, and that's bad." She also observes that "there's so many guys in the computer science classes that ask the dumbest questions. It's always OK for them."

Another woman comments that "It is a testosterone thing that you can't ask for help with computers. You can't admit that you don't understand something." For instance, whenever Lori asks a question of a male with another major, he retorts, "What's your major again?" She describes reading an assignment and feeling she didn't even know where to begin and "not having any urge to ask my peers." She said, "I would go to my TA, but even that wouldn't be the greatest feeling . . . because it would be like a 'Well, what are you doing here?' feeling." So she sits alone with her questions.

When we ask one female student how statements like "you got in just because you are a woman" affect her, she shows the spirit of resistance that pulls some of these women through: "Well, we just say 'Don't say that!' It does hurt to hear that, but we don't really pay any attention to them. . . . They are not worth paying attention to."

The Need for Respect and Support

In his article "Race and the Schooling of Black Americans," Steele argues that a critical component of reducing the vulnerability of women students in traditionally male fields and of African American students overall is for the student to feel "valued by the teacher for his or her potential and as a person." He considers building a relationship of respect between teacher and student for women and minority students to be "the first order of business—at all levels of school. No tactic of instruction, no matter how ingenious, can succeed without it" (p. 77).

Unfortunately, this quality of relationship between faculty and undergraduate students is far from universal. We found at Carnegie Mellon that a few exceptional faculty, serving both as instructors and as advisors, served as valuable anchors for students during the first year and especially the first semester. Beyond that, though, many students felt they were "pushed out of the nest" and left to fly on their own. While many students formed bonds with other classroom teachers, research advisors, and departmental advisors, for many others no other relationships with faculty took the place of these first-year ties. Women students, especially, noted the absence.

Seymour and Hewitt's (1977) cross-institutional study underlines the importance of faculty mentorship relationships for women students. They stress that "failure to establish a personal relationship with faculty represents a major loss to women, and indeed, to all students whose high school teachers gave them considerable personal attention and who fostered their potential" (p. 267). They found that the relationship between teachers and students is particularly significant for female students, for "to be faced with the prospect of four years of isolation and male hostility on the one hand, and the abrupt withdrawal of familiar sources of praise, encouragement, and reassurance by faculty on the other" is particularly discouraging

(p. 271). They found that "more women than men arrived in college with the expectation of establishing a personal relationship with faculty" (p. 267).

Seymour and Hewitt (1997) also found that women objected to large classes because "you don't get to know the professor," faculty are "too impersonal," and "the professor doesn't care about you" (p. 267). Men, in contrast, objected to large classes because they have "negative effect on grades," encourage more competition for grades, and are usually taught by less qualified faculty.

Researchers Amy Zeldin and Frank Pajares (2000) found that

the most important factor in the enhancement of self-efficacy beliefs of women in mathematics-related careers was the confidence that significant others expressed in the women's capabilities. . . . Women seemed to rely extensively on the accompanying confidence development from the relationships in their lives while they were honing their mathematics-related skills. Relational episodes gave birth to relational confidence developed from others, and this relational efficacy informed their judgments of their own abilities profoundly. (p. 239)

Considering the peer dynamics, the computing experience gap, and the technology-focused curriculum that is all too common in computer science programs, it is not surprising that faculty mentoring and social relationships can play key roles in women's persistence.

The Decision to Leave

In our study, we had the privilege and pleasure of talking with women students who overflowed with interest in computing as they began their college careers. Cecily, a bohemian type, dreamed of making computerized gizmos and gadgets, "techie Jim Henson puppets." Maura's interest was in biogenetics and computing. For those of us on the research team who were social scientists, who admittedly held our own preconceived notions of who is or isn't thrilled by computers, it was an eye-opening experience to sit with woman after woman and have her relay her enchantment with majoring in computer science.

Our initial conversations with these women, who were just beginning their studies, were filled with exclamations about learning computer science. By the second or third semester, it seemed as if we were talking with different people. No longer buzzing, too many of these women students now were questioning whether they were still interested. The spark in their eyes had faded; their flame of interest was dull. It happened so very quickly. And it happened time and time again. It was very disheartening.

During the first year of our research, six of the seven first-year women made the dean's list. The picture became more complicated and less rosy in the second year. Of the seven female students of the 1995 first-year class, four had left computer science by the second year. (One has since returned.) Of those four, two were top students. Among the 1996 cohort of fourteen first-year female students, three students had transferred out of CS within the first year. In the second year, seven began to question seriously whether they would remain in computer science. From our sample of twenty-nine males, three have transferred to other departments, and three (two African American and one Hispanic) have left Carnegie Mellon. Of the female CS majors who have transferred out, multiple factors were involved, the two predominant ones being lack of interest in the course material and self-questioning of their ability, often in relation to their peers.

Attrition of women from computer science has been a significant problem both at Carnegie Mellon and nationwide. Women in the computer science program have transferred to other majors or left Carnegie Mellon at more than twice the rate of male students over the past several years. While it may be tempting to assume that the difficulties expressed by women who leave the program are somehow unique to them, in fact the majority of women in the program, both those who leave and those who stay, express similar dissatisfaction with their peers, the culture of the discipline, and the teaching. The persisters go through the same processes of self-doubt, fear, and anxiety as the leavers. Seymour and Hewitt's (1997) study also found that the experiences and attitudes of those who stay are not very different from those who leave:

Perhaps the most important single generalization arising from our analysis is that we did not find switchers and non-switchers to be two different kinds of people. That is to say, we did not find them to differ by individual attributes of performance, attitude, or behavior to any degree sufficient to explain why one group left, and the other group stayed. (p. 30)

Conclusion: The Responsibility to Change

Our analysis of the nexus of confidence and interest leads to an emphasis on institutional responsibility. We do not blame the student or expect her to toughen up, turn a blind eye, or adjust. We believe that educational institutions and their culture, curriculum, faculty-student relations, norms, and standards must change. The problems of teaching, faculty and peer relationships, models of success, curricular focus, and the experience gap all work to the detriment of women's interest in computing. We believe that the decline in women's confidence must be acknowledged as an institutional problem. It is all too common for these psychological concerns to be regarded as beyond the purview of developing a strong computer science curriculum.

It is also too easy for faculty and administrators to take at face value the reports of many students who leave a major due to "loss of interest" and to view this as a natural course of events. If they are unaware of the complex relationship between interest and confidence, they may simply conclude that those who leave are (in Seymour and Hewitt's term) "appropriate switchers" (p. 392): they have found their intellectual interest and passion elsewhere. It is only through understanding the processes by which many women experience an unwarranted loss of confidence, leading to a corresponding loss of interest, that institutions can prepare to intervene.

Seymour and Hewitt also found that in the absence of institutional intervention to actively support women students, what distinguished the persisters from those who left was "the development of particular attitudes or coping strategies" (p. 30). In the following chapter we look at the qualities, experiences, and personal strategies that allow women to stay (and sometimes thrive) in the face of alienation, doubt, and uncertainty. We focus on what the women students who persist as a small minority in the computer science major over the four years reveal about how they sustain confidence in themselves and interest in the subject.

6

Persistence and Resistance: Staying in Computer Science

The Persistence Roller Coaster

During our research we were often surprised by which students stayed in the program and which left. Especially in the first two years, many women ride an emotional roller coaster of certainty and doubt from term to term, indeed from week to week, and whether they decide to finish the ride or get off before it ends is unpredictable. Although we interviewed students each semester, students' decisions to leave the program or to stay surprised us more than once.

Paula, for example, began the program excited, enthusiastic, and confident. She had completed a summer internship at one of the local computing labs and was enthusiastic about majoring in computer science. But not long after her arrival, she began to have doubts about her interest and abilities and started talking about leaving. The following semester she told us she had decided to stay, was happy in the program, and was sure she would continue. In her third semester, she told us she had decided to transfer out because "it just isn't worth it" any more.

As often as we were unprepared when women who seemed happy left, we were also sometimes surprised to find them staying. In *Talking About Leaving: Why Undergraduated Leave the Sciences*, E. Seymour and N. Hewitt also refer to this back-and-forth dynamic of students' decision-making process. The one thing that did become predictable was timing: students would most likely leave in the sophomore year, the time when most students, across all majors, do their switching.

What determines whether a woman chooses to stay in or leave computer science? In this chapter we look at what we call the pillars of persistence— the qualities, experiences, and strengths that allowed the women we interviewed to persist despite doubt and uncertainty. We are particularly intrigued with the counterintuitive stories of some of the women students. While a segment of the female persisters resembles the majority of men in certain ways, the portraits of many successful majors run contrary to expectations and assumptions about who can and will succeed.

The Expected: "I Have Always Been Around Computers"

One may intuit that women who persist are likely to come from backgrounds similar to many of the males: computer-intensive families, lots of parental support, a fair share of hands-on experience, fascination with computers. But one of the most surprising findings of our research is that the backgrounds of the women persisters varied wildly. Brenda is someone whose background is similar to what we've described, except that her family includes female role models. She describes her family as "basically a whole family of nerds." Brenda has had computers in her house since she was in kindergarten. The whole family used them, and they often had several going at once. As a result, she says computers and her interest in them are "natural" to her. Brenda's dad is an engineer, her mom is a librarian, and her sister is studying computer science at MIT:

So I've always been around computers, and it's just . . . natural to me. Even when we first had an Apple, they'd [parents] encourage me to just pick up stuff and try around. . . . We'd do it cold—do it without a disk—and I started programming in Apple Basic, just very simple stuff, and it got me interested in it. So everything else later just came naturally that I wanted to learn about.

Brenda's family didn't watch TV much, and computer games were her entertainment. She "dabbled a bit in Apple Basic to see what fun stuff I could do," learned word processing, and did her science projects on the computer. Her parents have lots of computer-literate friends, and when they visited, they would all play computer games together. In junior high, Brenda started getting involved in the Internet through her sister and mother. She helped run bulletin boards. She also had friends who used computers, though not as much as she.

Brenda's "family of nerds" helped her sense of fit and belonging in computer science. Computers were part of her furniture; they became "natural" to her. Perhaps unsurprisingly, Brenda describes her decision to major in CS as a "kind of a default." She had a wide variety of interests, from music to math to writing, "so it was kind of a toss-up of what I really wanted to do." But she decided that she was "probably the most comfortable around computers in general." She adds, "I'm not sure exactly what area I want to go into. I only know . . . I like computers. So that's a good place to start." Even though she found many of her classes very challenging, Brenda is satisfied with how she did in all of them. She enjoys learning to write code. She says, "I know how to think like a programmer." But she adds, "I'm also not a super-genius or anything."

Family make-up emerged in our study as worthy of further investigation. As in Brenda's case, we repeatedly heard women with no brothers attribute their interest in computer science to this fact. While we do not have enough data to draw a firm conclusion, we heard many reports of boys claiming the title of "family computer wizard," with this spot seemingly opening up for a girl in families with no brothers.

The careers and interests of a student's parents also have a major influence on whether a woman pursues an interest in science or engineering. Not only do women with parents in technical occupations pick up language and concepts around the dinner table, but the intimidation factor decreases, and parental mentoring and encouragement increase. The impact of parents is documented by Paula Rayman and Belle Brett's (1993) Pathways Project, a longitudinal research effort at Wellesley College that investigated the experiences of young women in science and mathematics during their undergraduate, graduate, and early career years. Rayman, Brett, and their colleagues found that parental support is one of the pivotal factors that distinguish women who go on to science careers from those who do not.

Coming from a computing or engineering family certainly provides important emotional and intellectual stepping stones for majoring in computer science, but our research shows that it is not required. Forty-eight percent of the persisters we interviewed did *not* come from "computing families." These students' stories provide us with an opportunity to find other stars in the constellation of persistence.

The Counterintuitive Persisters

Some of the most fascinating stories of persistence were told to us by women students who had absolutely no computing experience in their family background. These were mostly international students, raised and educated primarily in countries other than the United States. (Approximately 30 percent of the female computer science majors at Carnegie Mellon during the course of our study have been international women—primarily from Asia and Eastern Europe.) Their motivations for choosing computer science, along with their lack of computer experience, make them the antithesis of the "computer-obsessed since childhood" stereotype. In fact, many of these women were only marginally interested in the field when they began the program.

From their experiences, we learned that despite the tremendous range of computing experience among students, women who are complete novices are no less likely to persist than the most experienced women. Their stories show us that prior computer experience does not make the critical difference. The portraits of these students fly in the face of expectations and assumptions about who can and will succeed in a competitive computer science program.

Little Experience and "No Choice"

Kanitha was a junior from Thailand. As one of ten children, her parents could not afford for her to attend university in Thailand. She came to the United States for high school, where she took her first computing class. Her decision to major in computer science was not based on prior experience or love of computing. She told us about her completely pragmatic, and in some ways very uninformed, decision to major in computer science:

Actually, I came from Thailand, and basically I hadn't dealt with any computer at all before I came. And after that I got a scholarship to study computer science, but I didn't know anything about computer science. And then I went to high school here, and then I started taking a course about computer programming, and it was kind of interesting. But then I mean, I have no choice, so that is why I am doing computer science.

Kanitha came to Carnegie Mellon on a corporate scholarship, which requires her to return to Thailand after graduation and work for her scholarship sponsor. She is very clear that the chance to study abroad is most important to her; what she studies is secondary. She eventually decided to choose computer science as a major over electrical engineering because the best scholarship offered was from the Bank of Thailand, which wanted computer science majors. We asked her why she chose computer science over electrical engineering:

Why? I don't know. . . . Actually, like the scholarship itself, you know, for this different scholarship I have a different sponsor for it, so after I graduate, I have to work for a different person. So now I am thinking about which one I want to work for. And then I finally ended up, "OK, I think I want to work for this sponsor." So that is why I picked computer science. It's not because of the difference between those two. I don't even know what the difference is. Because I have to go back and work, so I just like consider the workplace and like the sponsor.

When asked, "How did you end up getting a scholarship to study computer science with no computer background?" she answers, "I just want to study abroad, so anything is fine with me." Kanitha has been an extremely successful student at Carnegie Mellon and is considering graduate school in computer science.

"You Have This Bridge You Have to Walk Over, and You Just Don't Look Down"

In another set of accounts, we hear how the pressing need of many international students to become breadwinners for their families leads them to pursue economic opportunity over personal interest. Concern for their families motivates them to stick it out and work hard despite doubt and lack of confidence.

Larissa, for example, moved to the United States with her family from Russia two years prior to attending Carnegie Mellon. She learned English while attending an American high school for two years. While Larissa had more prior computing experience than did Kanitha (she used to play computer games with her dad), she had little experience in comparison to either men and women from the United States. Throughout her four years at Carnegie Mellon, Larissa consistently ranked at the top of her class. She was thoughtful in reflecting on her experiences learning to live with the computer culture, accepting how little she knew compared to the peers around her.

Larissa described her first two years as walking over an "abyss." It was very difficult for her, and she frequently doubted herself:

You have this bridge you have to walk over, and you just don't look down. . . . There were cases when I started looking down, and it was really scary. I'd think,

"WHY am I putting myself through this?" . . . But I have to do this, anyway, because I have to.

Larissa felt there was no option for failure, since her entire family was counting on her for financial support. Her father had been a research scientist in Russia, but in the United States has been managing a small restaurant. Her brother's ability to go to college depends on the money she will make after graduation. She has no financial safety net beneath her and feels she must persist. She believes that "you cannot have everyone doing what they want to do," that there is "supply and demand with jobs and what needs to be done," and that "basically, we have to do good to stay here." And she adds, "It's just a matter that if I'm doing something, I have to be good at it, so . . . you just work hard."

Degrees of Freedom

Motivations like these can boost persistence of students, even in less than ideal circumstances. Seymour and Hewitt (1997), in *Talking About Leaving,* speculate that "gender differences in perceived degrees of freedom to choose and to change direction" lead more women than men to leave the sciences (p. 278). They suggest that especially among students from socially and economically advantaged backgrounds, women choose disciplines "largely by the degree of personal satisfaction they offer" and "pay less regard to their economic viability" (p. 279). The result is that when the math-science tightrope becomes culturally or academically uncomfortable, women with safety nets may jump: "Reports of relatively easy release from initial commitment to a science, math, or engineering major were most common among women from economically advantaged families" (p. 278). On the other hand, Seymour and Hewitt found that black women, older women returning to school, and women from working-class families did not feel the same degree of freedom. We found this also to be the case with many of the international women students.

We do not advocate that women forgo personal happiness and sacrifice academic pleasure in the interest of expediency or financial incentives; rather, we are pointing to ways that motivations can affect persistence. But what also is required is a strong sense of self-efficacy. From interviews with these counterintuitive persisters we were able to identify several "pillars of persistence" that help boost students' sense of self-efficacy.

Attributional Beliefs about Intelligence and Talent

Research on learning motivation based on U.S. students has found that students generally hold one of two opposing views on intelligence. One view is that intelligence is a fixed trait—as in "you are born with the talents that you have, and nothing you do can change them." Students who hold this view tend to focus on performance issues such as grades and other forms of external approval. The other view holds that intelligence is a malleable quality—as in "if you work hard and practice, you will improve." These students tend to orient toward learning goals such as improvement and developing mastery.

Which of these dueling views a woman in computer science holds can make a difference in her sense of self-efficacy and persistence. The research of psychologist Carol Dweck (1986), who studies learning motivation, shows that "a focus on ability judgments can result in a tendency to avoid and withdraw from challenge, whereas a focus on progress through effort creates a tendency to seek and be energized by challenge" (p. 1041).

Believing in the link between effort, hard work, and success seems to be the mantra for many of the international women students. A woman from Thailand, in describing her first-year experiences, credits hard work for her success:

I know it's hard, it's really hard, because I remember my freshman year. I want to give it up because it's hard. But then I thought, "That's a loser's talk." So then I should try it and work hard. I think I can do it.

An Indian student attributes her persistence to "lagan," a Hindi term akin to "putting your nose to the grindstone." Using an example from Indian math education and its routine disciplined drills, she connects her cultural and educational training to her success in computer science:

But that routineness, I think, is something that isn't taught enough here. . . . And so people here have, from my experience with my classmates, I see they have a lot of insight, a lot of intelligence. . . . You know, they [snaps finger] pick things up as quickly, but they don't have the grit to sit down with something for, say, six hours and say, "All right, I'm going to get this done no matter what."

When we ask Larissa what factor she feels contributed most to her success, she tells us, in no uncertain terms, that it was "hard work." She believes that despite knowing less than other students, she will catch up and succeed by working hard.

Culturally Inscribed Attributions of Success

Psychology professors Harold Stevenson and James Stigler (1992) have conducted a cross-cultural examination of beliefs about achievement. Their research aimed to figure out why American children seem to be forever losing educational ground compared to children in some Asian countries. In their book *The Learning Gap: Why Our Schools Are Failing and What We Can Learn from Japanese and Chinese Education,* they examine the organization of schooling and the practice and profession of teaching. They also look at attributions of success and show how these beliefs are culturally inscribed.

Stevenson and Stigler (1992) consider the prevailing philosophies in Asian cultures and note that Confucian philosophy promotes the belief that lack of achievement is due to insufficient effort rather than to a lack of ability or to personal or environmental obstacles. In other words, a person who works hard will master a task. Many Asian students grow up hearing adages like those of Chinese philosopher Hsun Tzu: "Achievement consists of never giving up. . . . If there is no dark and dogged will, there will be no shining accomplishment; if there is no dull and determined effort, there will be no brilliant achievement" (p. 97).

In elementary schools throughout China, young children hear parables instructing them to work hard, put in the effort, and learn. One such tale is about Li Po, a poet who walks by a small stream and sees a white-haired old woman who has made a needle from a rock. The woman advises Po: "All you need is perseverance. If you have a strong will and do not fear hardship, a piece of iron can be ground into a needle." Other sayings and mottos convey the belief in hard work and effort, such as "The rock can be transformed into a gem only through daily polishing," and "the slow bird must start out early" (Stevenson and Stiegler 1992, p. 98).

Suzuki, the early childhood educator who introduced a now world-famous method of teaching the violin to very young children, had a similar philosophy about children's learning. Teaching violin to young children is not a question of seeking out the naturally talented. Suzuki (1978) believed that all children, with daily practice and hard work, could learn to play the violin. A boy or girl does not have to be a child prodigy to learn to play very young. Suzuki's teaching model compares violin playing to language acquisition: it happens through regular practice and repetition at a very young age.

Jane has read her daughter the story of Lilia, the 1996 Olympic gymnastic gold medalist from the Ukraine. In the official version of the Ukrainian gymnastic federation, Lilia is not a "natural" gymnast. Her hands are too small for the bars, and her back is weak. But Lilia's coaches recognize her determination—"a will to win and work exceptionally hard." Almost every section of the book repeats this refrain. The book also describes how it takes a team effort of Lilia, her coach, and her choreographer to win the medal. None of them could do it alone. Rather than the single famous star, the book is about a team that works hard until it wins.

Hard Work Versus the "Computer Gene" Theory

When faced with difficult course work, American women also work hard—very hard. Yet too quickly they hit bottom, concluding that they lack the "natural and innate talent" with which the men seem to be born. Lily, a U.S. student who was full of enthusiasm when she began a year ago, in her last interview questions whether she should be in the program:

I don't really feel like I should be in the department. What am I doing here? So many other people know so much more than me, and this just comes so easy to some people. . . . It's just like there are so many people that are so good at this, without even trying. Why am I here? Do I want to work my butt off for four years, when there are so many people that it comes naturally to? Should I be here for the sake of the field even? You know, someone who doesn't really know what she is doing?

Lily ultimately despairs, concluding that no amount of practice or time spent on a task could improve her mastery of the material. As another female student says:

There are people who are born to do this, and I am not one of them. And it's definitely not one of those things that, like, "Oh, with practice, you will become one who is born to do it." . . . I think a lot of people are just born with it. You just gotta be like, "Computers! Yeah! they are awesome!! They are my life!" You know, a lot of computer scientists, that's all they do.

We continued to hear this refrain, as women looked around and experienced their male peers knowing more and doing the work with greater ease. We have found too many American women fall victim to the "computer gene theory," even if unconsciously.

Gender and the Entity View of Intelligence

In her article "Motivational Processes Affecting Learning," Carol Dweck (1986) suggests girls may be more likely than boys to subscribe to an "entity" view of intelligence—seeing ability as a fixed, static trait—and therefore exhibit a tendency toward low expectations, challenge avoidance, and debilitation under failure. She describes a series of studies by Leggett who assigned a novel "concept formation task" to bright junior high school students (Leggett 1985). Researchers observed a greater tendency of those girls who subscribed to the "entity" view to avoid challenge.

The entity view of intelligence can take its toll even on a student who works extremely hard. We witnessed how a student who attributes her math success to hard work rather than ability can have low expectations for future success precisely because she thinks her future courses will be even more difficult and demanding than the ones in which she is currently enrolled. A top student in her class reasoned that her As were the result of hard work, not ability; in her view, others got As without working so hard. Despite her 4.0 average, she ended up leaving the major, convinced that she was ill-suited for the field because she put in so much effort.

Cultural Resistance

In chapter 4, we discussed how the male hacker has become the cultural norm in computer science, the standard to which women students begin to compare themselves. We have found that women who persist are those who find a way to get grades they are satisfied with and who can develop a personalized view of computing and their place in it. Women who accept the prevailing culture as the norm and who continuously compare themselves to this norm and find themselves coming up short are the ones who suffer the most.

The majority of women struggle to find a place where they can feel comfortable in the prevailing culture. One female student told us how she has refused to conform to the image of the myopically focused "computer geek." And since she is "getting really good grades without changing myself," she is ever more confident that she can remain in the major and be herself. When the interviewer asks her if she feels any need to conform to the culture around her, she answers:

I refuse to. I was worried what if I don't. Will I need to conform to that? Will I need to read books on computers all of my free time or something to survive here? And I feel so far I haven't. I'm getting really good grades without that . . . without changing myself. So I feel much more confident now that I don't have to. It's kind of nice. I can prove them wrong or something.

Ironically, it is in this area of relationship to the culture that the international women may have an edge. The international women do not as readily use the U.S. male hacker as their reference group. Since they are not fully part of this culture, their reference group is elsewhere. Many international students have alternative success norms and social bonds that protect them. Other priorities are dominant, and with these come other scales for self-evaluation.

It is important to note that some women students do feel the prevailing culture is a relatively good fit for their interests and personality. They take pleasure learning to walk the walk and talk the talk; becoming part of this culture helps them persist. An American female student talks of a sense of mastery when she became familiar with computer science (CS) jargon: "It kind of feels like becoming part of a club—CS club." She observes that her new adopted lingo may not be required but that "it is what you grow into:"

I've had several friends who are walking along the sidewalk and make a joke and say it in code. It's something that non-CS people or maybe an arts person would just think is totally stupid, but we think it's funny. It comes naturally.

Another woman reports, *à la* Star Trek, that "resistance is futile" and takes pleasure in the thought.

Breaking the Isolation and Building Support

"Surround yourself with supportive people!" is the mantra of a current American graduate student who attended Carnegie Mellon as an undergraduate. She attributes her undergraduate survival to the support she received from her family and friends. She recently tells of being the only woman in her lab in graduate school. She didn't mind that except that there was a "guy in the lab who was a sexist pig, to put it nicely." She describes the support she got from the other students in the lab:

But the best part of it all was that any remarks he made would be stifled by the other men in the lab. I had good friends! They were shocked at this guy, and he shut up (and thankfully left school) eventually.

Rebecca, a junior, tells us that her boyfriend, "can't really help me with my assignments, but he's good moral support." She describes him as "one of those people who, when I am saying 'I can't do this assignment anymore!' he's like, 'Yes, you can. I know you can. I've seen you do these things before!'"

Vera, a junior, talks about the support she received from a computer science women's dinner. She begins by describing her earlier social isolation, being one of a minority of women in the midst of male bonding:

Being female is scary in this program. First you feel alone, and you don't know who to go to, and you don't know who to talk to. You just feel weird because you see the immediate bonding between other people, just male bonding . . . just showing off and talking. . . . I can still get intimidated easily. And you just feel like you're in a minority. It's just a weird feeling.

She then describes how her self-doubt turned around when she attended her first dinner for computer science women students. She realized that others shared similar feelings and she was not alone:

I had all those feelings, and I didn't think that anyone shared those. I remember we had a CS dinner with the women in grad school. And it helped me a lot because I wasn't talking, but I was listening, and I thought everybody was saying the exact same things that I was feeling . . . like everybody was talking about them. And it was a big relief for me to realize that actually other people, other females were feeling the same way. And I just felt so much better. I remember after feeling . . . it was such a big relief.

Chirudee, a Thai student, also notes the importance of having a support network of friends. It was the presence of many Thai students on campus that convinced Chirudee to come to Carnegie Mellon in the first place. And indeed the Thai social circle turned into her support network. She says she pulled through one of her difficult programming classes and even enjoyed it because her friends were also taking the course:

I kind of enjoyed it. But not many people enjoyed this class. But I did because there were many of my friends taking it and we would kind of like suggest with one another. And then I felt like fun doing it, so I mean I enjoyed it. The instructor . . . I felt he was OK. . . . I mean he wasn't that great. But my friends didn't like it, but . . . because of my friends I kind of enjoyed it.

Supportive Learning Communities

Salina grew up in Malaysia and has ten brothers and sisters. Both her father, a forester, and her mother, a housewife, were computer illiterate. She attended a boarding school and was in the "science track." When she arrived at Carnegie Mellon, she "knew a bit about Basic, and I had never really done any hard programming work at the time." She rated her preparedness at the time of beginning Carnegie Mellon as two on a scale of five and had low confidence. By her junior year, she rated her preparedness as a four and her ability as a three.

Salina describes her first year as a "really hard year for me." Her confidence was low, and "I see all these other students just grasping the concept in less time that I could." She sat in class, feeling lost and "in shock," feeling that maybe she couldn't make it. She says, "I was just totally scared at the time." But she says, "just by working harder I eventually caught up with the whole class, and I ended up getting an A in the class."

Salina attributes her success partly to the support she received from friends. She said that everybody was just helping each other out. In her second semester she took 15–211, the course with a reputation of being a major hurdle:

I was really just baffled in that class because I just couldn't understand anything, so my confidence went down again at that point, plus I didn't know anybody in that class. So I dropped the class because I didn't have any confidence in doing that. . . . I took the course again in sophomore year, and things started to get clearer for me. Understand things better, plus at the time I made a lot of friends in the major. And you know, it is just the feeling that you have people going through the same thing with you. So it makes it better.

Former University of California calculus professor Uri Treisman (1992) believes that a supportive learning community is critically important for the success of minority students in math and science. Seeking answers to the high failure rate of African American students studying calculus at the University of California at Berkeley, Treisman observed that Asian American students formed social communities in which they helped each other with math, competed at mastering the material, and generally supported each others' learning, similar to what was described by Chirudee above.

He also found that most African American math students he studied were highly motivated, worked hard, and studied long hours but that even the best-prepared among them were failing. What stood out between the Asian and African American students was not a difference in motivation, preparation, or family support but in integrating studying and learning into social lives. African Americans were academically isolated and did not congregate into learning social communities the way the Asian students did. Instead, their academic interests and social interests were separate while they worked hard (and somewhat unproductively) on their own.

Observing the extra boost that comes from living and engaging with the material, Treisman has formed communities for African Americans similar to those created by Asian American students. These communities are built around intellectual interests (in this case calculus), provide well chosen problem sets that drive group interaction, and foster a supportive learning environment. Currently, Treisman-inspired Emerging Scholars programs operate in numerous colleges and universities and achieve high rates of retention in calculus courses among African American and Hispanic students.

Computer Science as an Acquired Taste

Studying the life arcs of women students in computer science over a four-year period has revealed to us some patterns of persistence. If students are able to stick it out through the second year, get grades they are pleased with, and reconcile their relationship to the culture, then their initial level of confidence often returns, accompanied by an increase in interest.

Interviews with persisters often reveal a key moment of success or achievement that keeps them going. For one senior, this moment was in her third semester, when she got over the hump of the data structures course (211) and began taking more advanced classes. She says that she had no confidence after 15–211 and "thought I would flunk out or get kicked out of CS." But then she ended up getting an A in the course that immediately follows in sequence (15–212). She is in awe that she mastered the more advanced material. And the fact that she did it on her own became very important for her. In 211 she frequently needed to consult her teaching assistant, but in 212 she "was able to go right through the course without help." That was her confidence builder:

> In 211 I was constantly going to the TA, and I was like, "I don't know how to do this!" And I felt like he was practically writing my programs for me because every time I'd have a bug or something, I'd be going to my TA two or three times for each program, at least. Then in 212 I was able to go right through the course without help or anything. It was just a great feeling for me, and I feel I learned a lot. And it was just a big transition for me. It was a lot of big "Ah-hah! So that's what we were learning before!" All of a sudden things started clicking. It was just like a really big transition for me.

While this feeling of self-sufficiency may seem contradictory to the confidence gained from working with a supportive group, one way or another students have to internalize a sense that they can do it. If students persist for a sufficient amount of time (at least through the sophomore year), the odds are that they will regain confidence in themselves. Brenda, a sophomore student, talks of this confidence:

But it's kind of like if you're running, and you get to this big hill, and you're like, "Oh man, I'll never be able to run up that." And you do, and then you get to the next big hill. So it's like you're not exactly dreading it because once you get to the top, you feel really good about yourself. I guess I used to be afraid of a lot of things, but as I keep getting over and over these courses that I never thought I could pass, I think I'm ready to do the next step. And I don't know how I'm ever going to do senior-year courses, but I'll know when I get there.

We have found that if students get through the first two years, that a sense of mystery about computing turns into a sense of mastery. Asked if her interest in CS had increased or decreased, one junior provides an example of an upward spiral of confidence and interest:

I think partly it's increased just because I put so much work into it. It's like when you invest this much time in something, you want to do good in it. And also, I think the more I learn the more I think, "I can do this thing!" I just need to work really hard at it. But yeah, I think I've gotten more interested in it.

A Malaysian woman describes the satisfaction she felt in sticking it out:

It's like an acquired taste for me. . . . At first it was very hard. . . . After a couple of years, I realized it's kind of late to back out. I sort of went through with it, and along the process I'm beginning to think I like it more and more. So at the end, I just went along with it, and it's pretty exciting, now that I learn more about it.

Conclusion

Despite doubts and uncertainties, women tend to persist in computer science when they reject and find alternatives to the dominant culture of the field. A larger question, though, is what institutions can and should do to eliminate the negative factors that lead students to leave computing programs. We touch on several ideas for high schools in chapter 7 and for universities in chapter 8.

7

A Tale of 240 Teachers

From 1997 to 1999, 240 high school computer science teachers gathered at Carnegie Mellon University to participate in the Carnegie Mellon Summer Institute for Advanced Placement Computer Science Teachers (6APT). The six Summer Institutes had a dual focus—to prepare teachers to teach the C++ programming language and to provide teachers with gender-equity instruction that would increase the numbers of girls taking high school computer science. Some 15 to 20 percent of the nation's advanced placement computer science teachers attended one of the six Summer Institutes.

Forty-six states were represented during the six sessions. Some teachers had Ph.D.s, some had left industry to teach; one was a home economics teacher who had been recruited by her principal to teach computer science because no one else in the school wanted the job. More than half were math teachers. Equal numbers of male and female teachers attended, a goal that is seldom achieved in training programs focused solely on gender issues. About 90 percent of the teachers were white, and their average age was in the early forties.

As part of their introductions, teachers reported the number of girls in their classes. Nearly a third had one girl or none in their classes. Several teachers said they hadn't realized how bad the numbers were until they had filled out the application to the Institute. We heard that computer science classes were not attracting top female students because "these girls have broader interests" and because they wanted to keep up their grade point averages. We heard that in some schools students decide by the ninth grade which AP courses they would take. One teacher talked about the counselors as obstacles in her school: "the counselors just don't think the girls can do well in the classes, so they discourage them from taking the courses."

Another teacher told of holding a "parents' night" to explain the computer science curriculum and finding that only parents of boys came.

While a few teachers in each session were familiar with issues of gender in computer science, most 6APT participants were examining the issue for the first time. It was clear that we were not preaching to the choir. Some teachers started out not realizing how severe the gender gap was, and others were downright suspicious of the Institute's intent but wanted to learn C++ at Carnegie Mellon. A big draw for these teachers was the opportunity to study C++ with Mark Stehlik, who has a nationwide reputation as a computer science instructor and AP reader. Another benefit was that the National Science Foundation sponsored the teachers' trip to Carnegie Mellon. This was an exceptional opportunity for teachers, who typically get few of the perks that are standard fare in other professional jobs.

A Singular Opportunity

In 1996, the Educational Testing Service announced that the advanced placement computer science APCS exam would be given in the programming language C++ starting in 1999. The exam had been given in the Pascal programming language since its inception. Most of the computer science high school teachers would now have to learn C++. Allan envisioned this as a singular opportunity to intervene in favor of gender equity: most of the approximately 1,500 teachers of APCS courses would need training in C++, as well as in appropriate pedagogy for the new language and its object-oriented style of programming.

We jumped at the opportunity to effect change at the K–12 level. Our first step was to build an interdisciplinary team. We asked Jo Sanders and Mark Stehlik to join us. Jo is one of the country's leading experts on gender and computers. She is the author of *Lifting the Barriers: Six Hundred Strategies That Really Work to Increase Girls' Participation in Science, Mathematics and Computers* (1994). Through a series of national training programs, Jo has taught gender-equity skills to thousands of teachers and teacher educators since 1983. She loved the idea of working with an interdisciplinary team and having a captive audience and signed on. Mark Stehlik, an extraordinary teacher of computer science at Carnegie Mellon and a reader for the AP exam, immediately saw an important opportunity.

Our interdisciplinary team was built. Allan and Jo wrote a proposal to the National Science Foundation and received funding for three years through the Program for Women and Girls, now the Program for Gender Equity.

The program's faculty would be joined in each session by two teacher assistants recruited from the group of high school teachers who grade the APCS exam as well as prior 6APT participants. These teachers would provide hands-on guidance with the programming portion of the program and also contribute their perspectives on classroom issues.

We modeled the institute after the interdisciplinary approach of our own research. The 6APT course would provide four key elements:

• Background information on gender issues in computer science, in technology-related areas, in the culture at large, and in pedagogical approaches;

• Technical knowledge of C++ and programming with objects;

• Specific skills and techniques for integrating C++ course materials (assignments, background lessons, and so on) with gender-sensitive pedagogy, classroom practice, and management of peer interactions; and

• Suggestions for creating change in the participants' home institutions.

Early in 1997, we advertised through the web and direct mail for participants for the upcoming Summer Institute. For the first session we received 120 applications for 80 openings. In the second year, we received 240 applications for 80 openings. We selected the participants based on their potential to increase the number of girls studying computer science in high school but also made an effort to select teachers from a diverse mix of schools. They included teachers from math and science magnets in wealthy districts in Illinois, from small rural schools in Alaska, and from large inner-city schools in Texas with mostly Spanish-speaking immigrant students.

Throughout each day, we conducted sessions both on programming and on gender equity. We worked hard to inseparably link programming instruction with gender-equity issues. As a result, participants were swimming in both streams each day. Having them continually dive from programming into gender and back again may have created choppy waters, but our intent was to make the point that these issues must become streams flowing into one another. We wanted to make sure that the way they learned C++ would model an alternative way of teaching programming that took a wide range of gender influences into account.

Laying Out the Problem

The opening sessions included an overview of gender socialization in homes and schools and how it impacts girls' trajectories in math and science. Each year we presented recent data on gender and science from the National Science Foundation that show how the math gender gap has narrowed but how women in science majors and in the technical workforce remain underrepresented.

Perhaps the most effective method of assessing the status quo was Jo's assignment to the teachers to perform research projects before their arrival at the Summer Institute. Participants presented their findings on the following topics:

• How many computer ads appear in girl and boy teen magazines? (Result: far more ads appear in the boy magazines.)
• Who purchases computers at homes? (Results: fathers and sons)
• Who speaks more in computing classes? (Result: males)
• What is the gender content of Saturday morning cartoons? (Result: boys are the strong heroes, girls are the helpless victims.)
• What are the gender models in textbooks? (Results: far more males are pictured.)

Teachers also called local teacher education programs to find out how many courses were offered in gender equity, called local high schools to get the gender breakdown for advanced math and science classes, and called the local school district to calculate the percentage of women who were teachers, counselors, principals, and superintendents. These research assignments were effective learning experiences that allowed participants to discover instead of simply listen to lectures.

Jo then debunked the common assumption that girls avoid computer science because of a particular "villain." While obnoxious boys, sexist male teachers, and discouraging counselors exist, she argued, they are not the main cause of the gender gap in computing. Rather it is often a cumulative effect of many lifelong gender socialization influences that discourage girls' participation. Students bring the gender gap into computer science with them as they walk through the high school doors. High school then compounds the existing problem. Jo emphasized that male teachers can combat this problem just as effectively as female teachers.

Why Girls Enroll and Why They Don't

Early in each Institute session, teachers generate two lists: one on why girls enroll in computer science, and the other on why girls don't. From year to year, the lists are remarkably consistent:

Why girls enroll
- Computing is useful in many fields.
- They have talent in and enjoy math.
- They have been personally encouraged by parents, teachers, or friends.
- They enjoy problem solving.
- They see great job opportunities.
- They have course requirements.
- Friends are taking the course.
- They enjoyed and succeeded in an earlier course.

Why girls do not enroll
- Courses are taught in a dry, abstract style focused on language details rather than applications.
- The classroom climate is unfriendly to girls.
- The course has too few girls.
- The course has a geeky reputation, and girls do not want to be associated with that image or with the people in the class.
- They fear they know less than others, and some of the boys reinforce that fear.
- Guidance counselors or parents actively or passively discourage girls from taking computer science.
- They fear ruining their grade-point averages.
- They have broad interests that result in scheduling conflicts, since computer science courses are often taught only in a single period.
- They subscribe to the stereotype that computing is a male activity.
- They find the games that are pervasive in the computer culture boring.

Throughout the week, the 6APT faculty presented research on these issues. For instance, teachers' observations that "girls are perfectionists" and that "girls get discouraged too quickly and give up too easily" were addressed. One teacher, in her application to the program, wrote this:

I see too many girls who seem to be much more worried about their grades than about learning. They seem to want to please the teacher rather than to branch out into new areas. They do their assignments, sometimes more faithfully than the males, but do not seek out ways to improve their work. They rarely have independent projects on which they are working. The males in the classes see themselves as successful when they make As, but they also see themselves as successful when they make Bs and sometimes even lower. Their comments may be "I really knew how to do that" or "that was a stupid mistake," or some similar statement that conveys their confidence in their ability. I have had girls with As and B+s say things like "I'm so stupid," and "I just can't do this," and "I don't understand anything we are doing." Yet it is clear by their comments and their work they have mastered the material. Girls with Cs generally never take another programming course. Yet boys with Cs often go on to the next course, and boys with Ds sometimes will try to go on to the advanced classes. I don't know what to do to change this. I would like to learn some techniques to be able to at least change it in my classes, in my department, and in my school.

Researchers of attribution patterns have found that boys often attribute their failure to external factors (such as a too-hard exam) and their success to their own abilities. The result is that they maintain their confidence even when they fail. But just the opposite is true for girls: girls tend to attribute failure to their abilities and success to external factors such as luck. As a result, any setback or difficulty can erode a girl's confidence in her abilities. This has profound implications for girls' risk taking and trust in their own judgment, important qualities in computer science. We shared this research (see further reading list) with the teachers so they could have a deeper understanding of students' behavior and could in turn pass this knowledge onto their students to better understand their own reactions.

What Teachers Can Do

We found that a little bit of discussion of the problem went a long way with the Institute's participants; they hungered for solutions. Much of the Institute's gender work, therefore, focused on the interactive discussion of solutions. As in the discussion of the problems, we drew as much on the teachers' hands-on expertise as on our own. We describe here some of the most important strategies that emerged over many hours of discussion. The quotes we use are from teachers' reports on what they did after attending the 6APT session.

Recruiting Girls

Boys have staked their claim at the computer very early both at home and in schools (See chapters 1 and 2). Girls who are interested but intimidated, or girls who don't quite know what computer science is but could be very interested, need an extra word of encouragement from teachers, parents, or counselors. Rule number one, then, is that *teachers have to deliberately focus effort on recruiting girls*. If teachers issue a generic recruitment call, boys turn out. Girls must know the teacher is talking to them. Sometimes all it takes is a few minutes of encouragement to fire a girl's interest and to give her the confidence to take a class.

Besides approaching individual students who teachers think will be interested, giving a recruitment talk in a math and science classes, while specifically mentioning girls, is a good idea. But so is going to history classes, where there are sure to be plenty of girls. Some teachers have reported going to the athletic teams and trying to recruit the entire team. Girls do not want to be the only one in the class, so two mottoes emerged: *"Recruit friendship circles"* and *"Recruit a posse."*

David Pevovar, an APCS teacher from Seattle, learned this about recruitment:

Actually, the discussions from last summer have been helpful with enrolling girls for next year. I have taken a new approach for recruitment of girls—that is, instead of visiting mainly chemistry and math classes when talking with students about next year's classes, I visited the AP U.S. history and honors world history classes, which usually have a larger female audience. Also, the local paper ran a nice article on the past successes of our female students and made a very positive comment about our program, which in turn created an interest in some parents in getting their girls involved.

He also observed,

The most important part is the personality of the instructor. You have to have a good relationship with students and actively pursue the students, especially the girls, and get them involved and show them that they can be successful. It's a lot of effort and hard work, and you can never sit back and say, "Just because I offer the class, they will come!"

Having Girls Recruit Girls

Teachers are very important for recruitment, but *some of the best recruiters of girls are other girls*. Nancy Mahosky, a teacher from Beaver

Falls, Pennsylvania, formed a gender-equity committee that organized senior girls in computer science to make a video about why they were taking computer science, why they found it useful, and why they liked it. The video featured a tour of the computer lab, interviews with girls who had taken programming classes, a discussion of what types of jobs involve computer science, and reasons that computing is important to learn. They then took the video to the middle school and gave a presentation to girls in math and science classes. It has been very effective.

Peggy Beninati, from Egg Harbor Township, New Jersey, increased her enrollment of girls from 9 to 25 percent over one year's time. She found that "the best recruitment tool was having kids talk with other kids":

I promoted next year's change to C++ using my star girl pupil. I went to calculus, AP calculus, and honor algebra classes targeting girls. I had my second-year students—including the boys—promote C++ to girls they thought would do well in programming. I talked to girls everywhere—in the cafeteria, in my classes, in anyone's class that would listen. . . . My current percentage of girls is 9 percent. Next year it will be 25.3 percent. I made flyers, gave speeches, stayed after school, talked students into talking others into taking the course. In the long run, I think that my best recruitment tool was having kids talk to kids—girls talk to girls, and boys talk with girls.

Another helpful hint emerged: *it is effective to recruit a "mover and a shaker,"* a girl who has strong links to groups of girls, such as a student government officer or a member of an athletic team. Teachers who are also coaches report that their greatest source of girls were the teams that they coached and that when one girl enrolled so did some others.

In a related vein Serita Scott, a teacher from Hamilton, New Jersey reported:

Another suggestion was to get a group of girls together in a committee or club to work with the guidance counselors and visit classes with them before scheduling begins. The girls will be the ambassadors for girls in technology. I approached girls who are in my AP classes and in the other AP teacher's classes and in my CS Club. They are enthusiastic about it and want to call themselves the Ambassadors Club. One girl with outstanding leadership skills has designated herself as mover and shaker of the club and recruited girls from last year's AP classes and two boys to become ambassadors.

Educating Counselors, Teachers, and Parents

Many school counselors, teachers, and parents don't know what is taught in a computer science class and how programming and other principles of computing are intellectual skills valuable across many disciplines. This was confirmed in a survey conducted by North Canton, Ohio teacher Deborah Wiley. She found that 66 percent of the students surveyed had no idea of what the field of computer science is all about; 13 percent believed that computer science is using the computer in science class; 8 percent believed that computer science is the repair and building of computers; and 7 percent believed that computer science involves programming and networking.

A frequent suggestion was to hold an open house to *explain to counselors, teachers, and parents what is being taught in computer science and why fluency in information technology is important* for students' future educational and economic opportunities. One teacher had the girls give the school counselors a tour and explain to the counselors what they got out of computer science. Teacher Judy Hromcik of Arlington, Texas, found the alliance with her school counselors paid off:

The counselors created a pamphlet that describes the courses entering freshmen and sophomores may take. They asked me to write the section describing CS. I included the information about the shortage of women in CS and how good the job market is for CS. The counselors loved this. They have been very supportive. My freshmen enrollment for CS went up from eleven to seventeen. In APCS, I currently have seventy-five students signed up and I think about thirty-plus females.

Getting Girls Interested Young and Early

Teachers report that among college-bound students, the trend for many students is to *plan electives and AP classes as early as middle school.* Middle-school students may also fail to take prerequisite courses if they are unaware of the choices that lie ahead. Several teachers reported taking their female high school computer science students to visit the local middle school or conversely inviting middle school girls to visit their high school classes.

"All-Girl" Computing Events

While all-female classes are generally not allowed in public schools, *girl-focused events, clubs, and camps can spark girls' interest in computing.* These events attract girls who would normally stay away from classes where they fear being left in the dust or shouted down by more experienced or just plain louder boys. They provide learning environments where girls take risks, take leadership, ask questions, stop worrying about what they do not know, and build their confidence.

Several teachers started all-girl events that have proven to be quite successful. Reva Power of Tomball, Texas, held an all-girl camp:

January 17, 2000, was a wonderful day for me. Seventeen eighth-grade girls attended a girls' computer camp. We worked with Karel++, had female speakers from the local community college talk about careers in technology, and had female speakers who have worked in industry using computers discuss the importance of computer science.

Pat Phillips of Janesville, Wisconsin, started the Dreams Project, which ambitiously targeted girls who were "at risk" for academic achievement but who teachers and counselors felt could make a real step forward with some mentorship and attention. The project involved parents as well as the girls and included a peer-to-peer mentorship program. Pat's strategy was to broaden the Dreams Project beyond computer science so she could ally herself with other teachers who also had a shortage of girls. Part of the project also focused on building girls' self-confidence and risk taking through a ropes course:

I'm giving myself an easy day today (i.e., lots of lab time) because last night was the first night of our peer-mentorship project between seventh-grade girls and eleventh-grade girls. We have fifteen of each. We literally drew names from a hat to match them and had an informally structured evening for them to get acquainted as well as mixer activities for the parents and professional women who have joined our forces. It went well. The parents of the seventh-graders were thrilled that this project has begun. The seventh-graders were selected because their teachers saw them as very bright but at risk of falling off the track because of peer-group friends, family structure, etc. We have decided to make these parents a target in the project also. We will be sending them occasional copies of articles, flyers for activities they might do as a family, etc. to increase their awareness of the problem and enlist their help in the solution. The help we received from the local AAUW has been outstanding. Also got (from local grant sources) all the $ we need for the next twelve months of activities, including a leadership outdoor weekend adventure trip (ropes course). We are enjoying this a great deal. The reception from all fronts has been quite spectacular.

Spreading the Word

Many teachers exercised their creativity on ways to *spread the word*. Several found that posting want ads for computer jobs on parents' nights sparked real interest among parents. Pat Phillips started the Stall Street

Journal, postings in all the school's girls', bathrooms: "I started a collection of brief news and magazine articles about gender issues. . . . we will copy a different one each week and hang them inside the stalls of the girls' bathroom."

Expecting Opposition

When teachers begin to make a special effort to recruit girls, they often encounter some opposition. Other teachers, boys, and sometimes girls may object that special efforts to recruit girls are not fair. One teacher reported the following situation:

> When they [senior girls] went to the Computer Club (fifty males, four females) to ask them to join [the efforts enroll more girls in computer science], no one did, and ten boys strongly objected to the whole project saying it was discriminatory against boys. Any suggestions for me here?

This is an important teaching opportunity: an opportunity to *explain how boys have already been recruited into computer science*. Public image, media, and marketing of computers have been specifically focused on boys. The gender stereotypes associated with computing tend to pull boys in and push girls away. To balance the influences, a concerted campaign to recruit girls is necessary.

Another form of opposition can arise from teachers and administrators who do not perceive gender as a high-priority issue in the face of many other demands on their time and attention. Many 6APT participants found that they were able to *enlist cooperation and assistance by doing some teaching* of their colleagues and superiors—sharing local statistics, nationwide statistics learned at Carnegie Mellon, and success stories reported by other teachers.

A third, and very difficult, problem that many advanced placement computer science teachers encounter is that *other teachers also wish to fill their classes*. The most common competitors faced by our group of APCS teachers were teachers of other advanced placement courses and teachers of business-oriented computing courses.

Reshaping the Teaching of Computer Science

Recruiting girls is a critical step, but if girls drop out regularly or have unpleasant experiences in computer science classes, nothing has been done about the computer science gender gap. In the second half of each Summer Institute, we focused our discussions on building a girl-friendly classroom. We addressed the following questions:

• What types of assignments will engage the interests of girls as well as boys?
• How can teachers address the unequal computing experience of boys and girls?
• How can teachers teach in ways that acknowledge girls' learning preferences as well as boys'?
• How do teachers ensure that a "boys' locker room" atmosphere does not dominate the computer science classroom?
• How can computer science be revisioned as a discipline so that it is meaningful for women as well as men?

To spark and engage girls' interest and engagement in computing, we believe that computer science must be viewed as a fully human discipline that, while highly technical, is linked to other arenas and people. Providing this broader vision of computer science takes thought and practice for teachers who have relied heavily on textbook programming assignments that involve dry, mathematical problems and male-oriented applications like sports statistics or missile trajectories.

During the Summer Institutes, groups of teachers revised typical textbook programming assignments, rewriting them so that they would better reflect a broader vision of computing. Teachers brainstormed a list of settings in which specific computer science concepts could be cast, selected one, and then brainstormed different ways to make an assignment on that topic engaging.

Allan provided a list of features for teachers to think about when designing programming assignments. This list reflects much of what is known about what many women find meaningful about computing (see chapter 3):

A Baker's Dozen Ways to Enrich a Programming Assignment
1. Make it useful. Encapsulate the principle being taught in a program a student might want to use, like a CD database or a list of friends' phone numbers.
2. Make it personal or local. Make a school map, a local business directory, or (in assignment 1) a program that prints the student's name in an interesting style.

3. Interface with other programs. Have students write their programs so they can exchange data with a spreadsheet, a database, or a web server.

4. Focus on ease of use. Help students understand the critical role that usability plays in software quality and reliability.

5. Use big data. Problems that are too large to solve by hand help students to understand the real value of computing.

6. Use real-world data. Have students find it and massage it into a useful form.

7. Use natural-language text. Students can write programs that manipulate or analyze large bodies of text retrieved from the web.

8. Make it sensory: graphics, audio, animation, manipulation.

9. Make it socially relevant. Build assignments around real issues like ecology, population trends, and so on.

10. Simulate! Simulating real systems (traffic, elevators, plant growth) brings computing closer to the real world and offers many avenues for creativity.

11. Include observations of the real world or of the program's behavior.

12. Bring in experts. A human being who can address either a technical issue or a computing application can be a powerful motivator. Experts can be "brought in" in person or over the Internet.

13. Illustrate how everyday computational objects work: calculators, remote controls, vending machines, elevators, Palm Pilots, and so on.

In response to the perception by teachers that their students (largely male) tended to focus too much on the speed of their programs and the speed with which they were able to write them, we also provided a list (by no means exhaustive) of additional goals for software design. These "ilities" are rarely appreciated by novice programmers, but almost always outrank speed in the real world and happen to be in line with many girls' connections with computing:

• Compatibility: working together with other programs.

• Composability: being able to be combined with other programs to create new, more complex programs.

• Durability: outlasting changes in surrounding systems.

• Extensibility: making it easy to add new features and functions.

• Flexibility: being able to operate in many environments.

• Maintainability: allowing programmers to make changes in a straightforward and reliable fashion.

• Portability: being able to run on multiple different systems.

• Readability: being comprehensible by somebody wishing to read and understand the program.

• Reliability: being free of bugs and capable of coping with unexpected conditions.

• Reusability: allowing reuse of program code in other settings and applications.

• Scalability: being able to run across many machines in a network with high efficiency.

• Usability: providing an intuitive and error-free interface to human users.

• Utility: providing a useful solution to a problem.

The Experience Gap

One of the Summer Institute high school teachers observed that by high school, many male students have such a high level of knowledge of software, hardware, and operating systems that they are immediately comfortable in class. For girls, it is often a different story: "When girls begin, they must first learn how to deal with the computer, the operating system, and the programs before they can begin to learn to program. This extra hurdle is sometimes overwhelming."

Can the teaching within a high school classroom take this experience gap into account and be tailored to a range of experience levels? Mark Stehlik, in his 6APT programming class with the teachers, acknowledged that the teachers were at different levels of computing experience and knowledge, that the goal was for each person to move forward, that no one would be moving at the same pace or speed, and that the point was just to learn as much and well as one could. Of course, in a high school situation, with grades at stake, this level of flexibility is much more difficult to achieve. But we believe this spirit can be evoked by the teacher in the classroom.

While collaboration and cooperative learning groups are often preferred and effective learning strategies for girls, the gender gap in experience between boys and girls in the computer science classroom makes it important to ensure that girls don't automatically fall (or be assigned by the group) into "support" jobs (such as data entry). A teacher wrestled with what she perceived as a downside of collaborative groups:

By allowing students to work more in groups, it became clear that many in the all-female groups (also some male students) became very passive about their learning and didn't push themselves as much individually to understand the material. They just waited around until somebody smarter (usually a boyfriend in another group) came along and rescued them (figured out their coding mistakes for them).

This teacher's observations raise the challenge of collaborative learning in computer science when there is a wide gender gap in experience. Can the more experienced students help the less experienced without acting superior and condescending? Can the less experienced accept help without feeling stupid, ignorant, or discouraged while making mistakes and asking questions? Are the girls in the class "waiting around to be rescued," or are they hesitant to appear stupid in front of their classmates? These peer dynamics must be carefully understood and then monitored by teachers. Further, it is also important to realize that it is not just girls who rely on friends to learn. Boys are continually swapping computing information with each other and looking to each other for assistance. Image to the contrary, they are not "lone wolves" in learning.

Protecting the Climate of the Classroom

Computer science classrooms often have the feel of a boy's locker room. The humor and the banter usually reflect the male demographics. Donovan Williams of Madison, Wisconsin, told us of a computer programming contest, organized by a recent high school graduate, that included problems titled "Don't Forget the Beer" and "Checkin' Out the Babes." He wrote to the contest organizer, explaining how the contest call assumed a male audience and could alienate female students. While cordial and tactful, his message was unmistakable:

Dear J,
I want to commend you on taking the time to organize and coordinate these programming contests during the year. You've done a nice job, and my students have enjoyed the opportunity to challenge themselves further. However, I have some concerns about the appropriateness of some of the problems for this contest. . . .
Your inclusion of "Don't Forget the Beer" and "Checkin' Out the Babes" has placed me in a difficult position. . . . It appears that you were trying to make the problems more interesting; however, you have made them inappropriate for a high school audience. Moreover, the "Checkin' Out the Babes" problem objectifies women, and given the lack of representation by females in this field (and in CS classes), this problem has the potential to do more harm than good. I have a female on my team, and I feel terrible that she may be exposed to this type of question—in an area where she is already a minority. All of this could be avoided with a little rewording. . . . Should these types of problems continue to appear in these contests, I

will probably have to withdraw any support for participation by our programming team members.

Mark Stehlik, while teaching C++ to the teachers, discussed how male humor and proclivities, such as excitement over blood and guts or sexist imagery, easily creep into classroom assignments and other computing activities. For one of the first programming assignments, Mark asked the teachers to use C++ to create a graphic display in the style of their male students. With this in mind, teachers programmed houses being burned and blown up. Mark acknowledged that these are the types of programs that get the "oohs and ahs" and the high-fives. He then discussed how to teach appreciation for programs that are as technologically sound and inventive, possibly more sophisticated, and probably more appealing to women students.

Classroom Conduct

We viewed a taped episode of *NBC Dateline* featuring Myra Sadker and David Sadker's research on gender dynamics in the classroom, focusing on the subtle ways that teachers' behavior in the classroom can shortchange girls ("Failing at Fairness," 1992). The film crew had visited the classroom of an elementary school teacher who considers herself a feminist. To the untrained eye watching this video, the classroom looked like a fair one. But the Sadkers pointed out how the teacher called on boys more than girls and addressed more follow-up questions to boys.

As part of the discussion on these classroom dynamics, we roleplayed with volunteer teachers as the students and Allan as the computer science teacher. Allan taught a lesson on "What Is the World Wide Web?" Not only did he address more questions to the men, but he shaped his lecture in a way that would spark boys' interests more than girls'. He presented a narrowly focused technical view of the Web, absent any discussion of its applications. In all six role plays, he devoted the lion's share of his attention and feedback to a male student. And despite knowing in advance what the game was, the female students became alienated by the discussion, felt they had nothing to contribute, and became silent. Teachers were surprised at the magnitude of the impact on the participants of seemingly subtle behaviors. After airing their reactions to participating in or viewing the role plays, teachers received checklists they could use to have colleagues monitor their own classroom conduct.

Action Plans

The culmination of the Summer Institutes was designing action plans that teachers could realistically carry out during the upcoming school year. The action plans addressed how teachers would actively recruit girls into computer science, how they would build alliances within the schools to address the gender gap, and how they would revise the curriculum and pedagogy so that once girls are recruited, they experience success and engage with the material. Teachers committed to the following:

- Speaking to math and science classes to recruit more girls,
- Reevaluating their programming assignments,
- Holding an informational discussion with counselors and an open house for parents,
- Starting a girls' computing club,
- Getting information about Ada Lovelace and Grace Hopper and displaying it in the classroom,
- Writing an article for the school newsletter,
- Holding a school assembly about computing careers and showing the breadth and social relevance of computing, and
- Speaking to that one girl who they had always thought would do great in the class but whom they had never approached.

Jo Sanders and Nancy Mahosky made suggestions for building alliances within the school so that they would not be doing all of this work alone:

- Form a Gender Equity Committee (or bring this issue to the existing Gender Equity Committee).
- Make an alliances with other teachers (such as the physics teacher or the wood shop teacher) who are interested in recruiting more girls.
- Make an alliance with teachers (such as the biology, art, and music teachers) who have many girls in their classes who could benefit from knowing computing but who rarely take computer science classes.
- Talk with representatives from the counseling staff, the principal's office, the dean's office, the athletic coaches, and the district so that they can help your efforts.

Conclusions

How successful have the advanced placement computer science teachers who attended the six Summer Institutes been? At this point, data are still being evaluated. We do know that all the 1997 teachers felt a year later that they had made an average of 2.5 changes in their teaching because of their participation in 6APT. The following changes were mentioned most frequently:

I have more awareness of my own behavior.	24
I make more of an effort to call on everyone.	21
I personally make an effort to recruit girls.	20
I have more ideas on how to work with girls.	16
I make sure I talk to current students as often as possible to help retain them.	13
I encourage girls.	10
I think about the issue of gender equity more.	9
I am more careful to use gender-neutral language.	9
I assign meaningful programs right away—less abstract, more real-life examples.	9
I provide more information on role models.	8

We also have some preliminary reports of achievements made by several teachers:

Egg Harbor Township, NJ	9 percent girls to 25 percent
McKinney, TX	5 percent girls to 31 percent
San Diego, CA	For the first time, more than one-third of the class is girls.
Fresno, CA	8 percent girls to 25 percent
Dayton, OH	Computer programming 17 to 34 percent; advanced computer programming 7 percent to 20 percent
Midland, TX	Pre-AP 13 to 27 percent; APCS I 31 percent to 51 percent

In July 2000 we received NSF funding to hold a smaller 6APT conference for those teachers who felt they had a "best practice" to share. At this conference, a principal was invited to accompany each teacher. We hope that having the principals attend will lend authority and support to the work that these teachers are engaged in.

The 6APT project embodied a unique collaboration: teachers noted how unusual it was for them to see computer scientists working in collaboration with feminists and social scientists. This collaboration had two major benefits. First, it enabled us to interweave gender-equity material with the presentation of technical material, helping the participants to use both together in their classrooms. Second, the prestige of Carnegie Mellon's computer science program and its close association with the APCS program gave credibility and appeal both to the training program and to the idea of gender-equity training among a segment of the APCS teacher population that might otherwise have been nearly unreachable. Most important, we were able to bring together a group of dedicated, hardworking, and imaginative teachers who are now positioned to make their computer science classrooms equally welcoming to boys and girls.

8

Changing the University

We intended our research into girls and women who study computer science to be not only an exercise in knowledge gathering but also a guide to action. Far from being a passive object of study, the Carnegie Mellon School of Computer Science has responded to our findings and other research with a variety of interventions, beginning soon after we launched the project.

Since 1995, the proportion of women entering Carnegie Mellon's undergraduate computer science program has risen from 7 percent (7 of 96) to 42 percent (54 of 130) in 2000. At the same time, persistence of female students remaining in the program until graduation has risen to nearly match that of men. This change has attracted a great deal of attention in academic computer science as well as in the general press. We have been asked many times, "How did it happen?" This chapter describes ways that colleges and universities can respond to the observations made in our research. While Carnegie Mellon's results rely in part on its particular circumstances, we believe that many of these interventions can be usefully employed in many settings.

We describe the interventions in two chronological stages: the first stage reflects actions taken approximately from 1995 to 1998 in response to the earliest results of the research project, and the second stage reflects developments that have taken place more recently. We review the overall impact of these changes on the enrollment of women in the program and consider issues for the future. We close with a discussion of implications for other institutions.

The Experience Gap

Perhaps our first realization on undertaking our research project was the magnitude of the computing experience gap between men and women. It was evident both in students' self-reports of prior experience and in the distress we noted among inexperienced women enrolled in the introductory programming course taken by all but the most experienced students. Although they generally performed well, they found it stressful to be in the same course with students who were far more experienced and also tended not to do as well in the next course.

Our first intervention, therefore, was to institute a curricular change that provided first-year students with four different ways to enter the curriculum, depending on their level of experience. One contributing factor to the success of this measure is the fact that the rest of the curriculum is neither tightly scheduled nor deep in prerequisites, so that students taking an extra semester to gain programming experience would soon "catch up" with other students and have an equal opportunity to take advanced courses.

Our initial approach was to design a course combining a discovery-based, real-world orientation with an introduction to programming, which would prepare students for a more advanced programming course. We also instituted a more advanced course for students with substantial prior experience. These changes increased levels of satisfaction among both more and less experienced students of both genders and indeed seemed to result in the smooth integration of the less experienced into the remainder of the curriculum. The School of Computer Science has recently evolved this arrangement into a flexible series of minicourses; results of the new arrangement are pending.

Admissions

Based on our observation that prior experience did not predict eventual success, it seemed clear that admissions policy should not give a strong preference to highly experienced students. Once we had made the curricular changes that allowed inexperienced students not only to succeed but to do so without extraordinary levels of stress, we set out to adjust admissions criteria to reflect this. This change, together with getting the message out to prospective students that "experience is not a prerequisite," helped to achieve early gains in recruiting women to the classes entering in 1996 through 1998.

More Attention to Good Teaching

We have noted in earlier chapters that good teaching is especially important to women because failures in pedagogy or in curricular integration affect women disproportionately. Our main effort in this regard was to use the teaching assignment process to put better, more experienced, and more senior teachers (note that these are not always correlated!) into the earliest courses of the curriculum, where women reported having the most distress. While this change had positive effects, issues of course size and articulation from one course to the next continued to cause trouble; these issues are still under discussion in the School as we write.

A second area of greater attention to teaching involved the integration of a unit on diversity, particularly gender equity, into the teaching assistant training provided by the School of Computer Science to its graduate students. The unit was created by Mark Stehlik, who supervised the TAs and conducted the training program. He worked with the university's Teaching Center to incorporate findings from our research and the open literature, as well as video footage of discussions among female students, into a session alerting TAs to the issues affecting women in their classrooms.

Contextualizing Computer Science

We have noted that a curriculum that places technology in the context of its real-world uses and impact is appealing to female students. Some of the elements of a contextual approach include

- Early experiences that situate the technology in realistic settings,
- Curricula that exploit the connections between computer science and other disciplines, and
- Diverse problems and teaching methods that appeal to a broad variety of learning styles.

We describe below some courses that exhibit these properties.

In 1994, we instituted an "immigration course" (IC) for students entering the undergraduate program. (The terminology comes from an

orientation course provided to incoming Ph.D. students for many years.)
The design of this course in fact predated our study and was inspired in
part by Sue Rosser's work in *Female-Friendly Science*. The course presented students with a broader view of computer science than they tended
to receive in their first few courses, which were heavily programming-ori-
ented. As organized by first-year advisor Jim Roberts, the immigration
course included a series of lectures by faculty from across the breadth of
the discipline, context-setting talks by the dean and associate dean, and information relative to students' adjustment to life at college. The IC seemed
to have its desired effect: while it was common for juniors we talked to
early in our study to say, "finally, I understand what computer science is
about," students who have been through the IC seem to have a much
clearer view of the field, its range, and its applications.

Three courses available to computer science students stand out as providing holistic project experience in an interdisciplinary group of students.
The earliest instance was the software engineering course. In an approach
pioneered by Bernd Bruegge, this course integrated its entire enrollment
(typically thirty to fifty students) into a single software development team,
complete with a management structure suitable to the project's scale. To
model a real project, Bruegge incorporated technical writers and marketing students into the team to participate in the process. The student team
worked with an outside "client" to define requirements, design a system,
and implement a prototype.

Dan Siewiorek took a similar approach in the design of his course on
wearable computers. The projects in the course integrated elements of industrial, mechanical, electronic, and software design. The student body
included students, both graduate and undergraduate, majoring in
appropriate disciplines. Again, the project teams typically worked in con-
cert with an industrial client.

A third example is Randy Pausch's course on designing virtual worlds.
In this course, Pausch calls on students' skills in software, scripting, and
graphical design. He stresses the interdisciplinary nature of this work by
selecting students not on the basis of their majors but on the basis of their
skills—what they could do rather than who they were. Students work in
teams of three, changing membership over the course of the semester, to
implement a variety of engaging virtual reality projects.

All three of these courses have been extremely well received and present
good examples of the integration of computing with other disciplines in

pursuit of real-world objectives. Unfortunately, all are appropriate more for upper-division students rather than for students in the first year or two of the curriculum; more attention to these concerns is needed in the lower-division courses.

A direct approach to the question of the social impact of computing is found in Computer Science in the Community, a course that engages students with nonprofit groups in the local community, applying their skills to community issues. Allan helped Joe Mertz and Kathy Schroerlucke of the university's Outreach Center launch this course, in part with the idea that it would attract female students. One of our early discoveries, perhaps obvious in retrospect, was that the maxim "if you build it, they will come" did not apply. Perhaps because they doubted their capability to help in a real-world situation, women registered for the course in disproportionately small numbers. Personal recruiting has improved the situation since.

All of these efforts provide paths for students to pursue in addition to the traditional, technically focused path. More remains to be done, especially in terms of early experience with integrated problems.

Culture

We have observed in preceding chapters that many students and faculty picture computer science students as narrowly focused, intense hackers. For students for whom this is not an appealing work style and whose career aspirations extend beyond narrowly technical work, this image can be repellent or discouraging. One of the aims of higher education must be to provide students with a broad picture of possibilities and to create an environment where alternate models are valued and respected. Faculty must be mindful of ways that the hacker culture becomes an ideal that is consciously and unconsciously promoted.

In light of these observations, we made some modest efforts to broaden perceptions of the field. Among faculty, this took the form of discussing the results of our research and that of others and introducing diversity considerations into discussions of curriculum and programming. Among students, in addition to stressing to entering students that prior experience is not a critical issue, we began to talk about achievement in computer science as more multidimensional than the standard "boy hacker" icon.

In the first two or three years of the project, we had a clear impact on the teaching faculty who are most in contact with first-year students. They became more aware of the difficulties women face, the gap in prior experience, and different motivations for entering the program. However, with a few exceptions, the tenured and tenure-track faculty, those who teach the higher-level CS courses and conduct computer science research, were less engaged at this point.

Outreach to High Schools

The Carnegie Mellon Summer Institute for Advanced Placement Computer Science Teachers (6APT program) described in chapter 7 was conceived with the goal of helping high schools and not of affecting Carnegie Mellon's enrollment. However, it did not escape our notice that teachers who formed a relationship with us might be more likely to send their gifted students our way. Indeed, the percentage of students in each class entering the School of Computer Science from 6APT schools has more than doubled since the beginning of the project. This is true for male as well as for female students. Over time, though, as 6APT participants have increased success at recruiting girls to their classes, we expect they will help to enhance the flow of women into Carnegie Mellon's and other universities' computer science programs.

Apparently Unsuccessful Interventions

Two categories of interventions that we attempted had no measurable effects. One was a variety of modest recruiting techniques, such as sending targeted letters to female admissions candidates and arranging for female faculty to make phone calls to the highest-ranked female admittees. While we cannot conclusively demonstrate that these measures had no effect at all, whatever effect they had was small.

A second category of low-impact efforts addressed the issue of establishing a community of undergraduate women students. On a number of occasions, even predating the research project, we and/or a female student initiated activities intended to bring women together for group discussion and mutual support. While the individual events were positively received, we were never able, in the early years of the program, to establish the momentum required for the activities to be self-perpetuating: whenever a student "sparkplug" emerged, she soon graduated or was consumed by other tasks. We may have never hit on the right formula for this style of activity, but we are inclined to believe that the limiting factor was the lack of a critical mass of women, resulting in a shortage of new leaders to take the place of those who left. Increases in the enrollment of women and the arrival of new faculty leadership have led to recent progress in this area.

Recent Developments and Current Activities

By early 1999, the issue of undergraduate women in computer science at Carnegie Mellon had reached a turning point. Jane was about to move to the University of California at Los Angeles. Allan had begun to work part-time with Carnegie Technology Education, an engagement that would move him out of his role as associate dean for undergraduate education by the middle of the year.

A timely development that year was the arrival at Carnegie Mellon of a new member of the SCS faculty—Lenore Blum, a longstanding advocate for women in the mathematical sciences. She has created and advises the Women@SCS Advisory Council (WSCSAC), a group of motivated and articulate undergraduate and graduate students in the School of Computer Science that meets weekly throughout the academic year. Blum's leadership has catalyzed an impressive outpouring of energy from the newly increased number of women on campus. Through the work of the Advisory Council, a number of important initiatives have been introduced:

• Continued monitoring and identification of curricular trouble spots, such as the transition from the introductory courses to the upper-level courses;
• Peer tutoring for students in 15–211, a course that has historically been problematic for women and novice computer science students; and
• A variety of events for women in the program to encourage cohesion and lessen social isolation. These include a dinner for women faculty and women students, a web page for women in SCS (www.cs.cmu.edu/~women), and a Big Sister/Little Sister program, in which computer science graduate students and seniors are paired with first- and second-year undergraduate computer science majors.

A project underway in the computer science Curriculum Committee is a reexamination of the undergraduate program's curriculum, informed in part by the WSCSAC. On the table are some of the issues we have noted regarding early courses that are better related to each other, more contextually integrated, and less technologically intense.

Another important development is that the growing number of women in the program and the highly visible activities of WSCSAC have led to increased awareness and interest in the faculty at large. Much word of mouth indicates that faculty are surprised and impressed by the newly increased numbers of highly talented female students. Peter Lee, Allan's successor as associate dean for undergraduate education, has also become a strong proponent of reform. He suggested in a talk to the faculty that the increasing numbers of women in the program would make the program even stronger and enhance its competitive advantage. Engaging the concern and involvement of a broader segment of the computer science faculty is an important step in broadening the culture of computer science and enhancing the appeal of the School to women.

One of the most significant changes for the 1999 to 2000 academic year was the revision, in late 1998 and early 1999, of the university Office of Admission procedures for admitting computer science students. These changes were, in part, a response to the urging of Raj Reddy, the former dean of the School of Computer Science, that admissions focus on applicants' potential to play leadership roles in computing.

The core of the change in procedure was to begin to place greater emphasis on applicants' nonnumeric attributes. Rather than just selecting the top 400 or so applicants with the highest grades and scores, the Office of Admissions began with a larger pool, all of whom would make excellent students, and then selected from this pool with the goal of building the best class. For example, applicants with demonstrated independence, energy, creativity, and community involvement were rated more highly than other students with equivalent grades and scores. Admissions counselors also were allowed to take economic, ethnic, and gender diversity into account in choosing the class. The result of these changes, given the strength of the School's applicant pool, was that the classes admitted and enrolled showed greater diversity than before, with no diminution in median grades and test scores.

Enrollment Results

The number of women entering computer science at Carnegie Mellon has increased dramatically since we began this project. The trend is illustrated

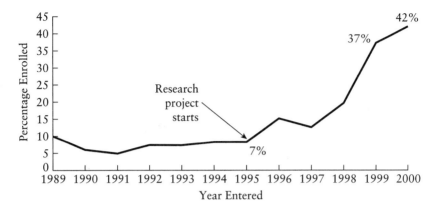

Figure 8.1
Enrollment trends for women entering the School of Computer Science

in figure 8.1. When we began the study in 1995, women made up just 7 percent of the incoming class. This number began to rise in 1996, and the increase has accelerated sharply with nationwide recognition of Carnegie Mellon's progress and recent revisions in admissions policy. The class entering in 1999 comprised 37 percent women, and the class entering in 2000 42 percent. These numbers are substantially above the national average, and approximately double the rate for comparable research universities.

We have also witnessed an increase in the persistence of women in computer science at Carnegie Mellon. Attrition of women from computer science has been a significant problem at Carnegie Mellon and nationwide. Women in the computer science program have transferred to other majors or left Carnegie Mellon at more than twice the rate of male students over the past several years. (This effect has been masked by the in-transfer of equivalent numbers, meaning that classes have graduated approximately as many women as have entered.) However, the rates at which both men and women leave the major have decreased over the past several years, and the persistence rate for women has begun to approach that of men. This trend is shown in figure 8.2.

We have been asked on occasion whether these changes represent an overall increase in the involvement of women in computer science or simply greater recruiting success by Carnegie Mellon at the expense of other institutions. Certainly improvements in student persistence help to make the pie bigger. It is harder to tell whether the women who come to Carnegie

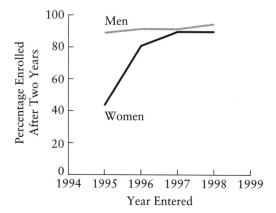

Figure 8.2
Persistence trends for students enrolled in the School of Computer Science

Mellon to study computer science would have done so elsewhere absent our program.

Should these changes persist in the long run, though, we have reason to hope they will contribute to the overall recruitment of women into computing in several ways. First, Carnegie Mellon's visibility and the attention its recruitment of women has attracted will encourage other institutions to undertake their own reform efforts; several such reports have reached us already. Second, perhaps more cynically, if institutions begin to find recruiting more difficult as a result of reforms undertaken by competitors, they will feel pressure to reach out themselves. Ultimately, though, we hope that individuals and institutions involved in reform of college education will contribute to a broader public vision of what computing is about, encouraging greater participation by young people of many different backgrounds.

The Challenge for the Future

The challenge that the School of Computer Science now faces is to make these recent enrollment changes permanent by maintaining or improving the enrollment and persistence of female students. While much of the early change has been induced by individual efforts and specific policies, history shows that such trends are easily reversed if not reinforced by systemic change. Our analysis, focused in chapters 3 through 6, points to specific

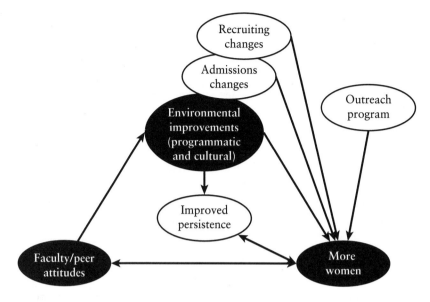

Figure 8.3
Creating lasting change in computer science departments

areas for change. Most of these areas are already under discussion by faculty and administrators at Carnegie Mellon.

Figure 8.3 presents a specific way to think about self-sustaining change. It shows that an initial increase in the recruitment of women can be achieved through a variety of programmatic efforts. The area of environmental improvements, which encompasses both programmatic and cultural aspects, is perhaps the most important factor that an organization can affect, as it is their main lever on student persistence.

The key to the longevity of these changes, though, is the recruitment of the faculty and students to continued environmental improvements. At Carnegie Mellon, the computer science faculty seem already to have had their interest sparked by the new presence on campus of large numbers of talented women students. If all of these influences are established, the full participation of women in the computer science program can become a stable, self-perpetuating process. If they are not, and if the enrollment of women continues to depend on a small number of contributors making targeted efforts, the change cannot be considered permanent or complete.

Implications for Other Institutions

A natural question is the extent to which results at Carnegie Mellon can be replicated elsewhere. The key distinction that Carnegie Mellon enjoys in contrast to many other institutions is its extremely competitive admissions. The importance of the ability to shift admissions criteria and the balance of a class with no discernible loss in quality of the recruited class cannot be underestimated. Nonetheless, based on our research and our implementation experience, we recommend several measures without hesitation to any educational institution.

The first is to pay ferocious attention to the quality of the student experience. As we discuss in chapter 5, women and other students who do not fit the prevailing norm are disproportionately affected by problems like poor teaching, hostile peers, or unapproachable faculty. Perhaps the most important place to start is the classroom experience. Early courses at many institutions use a "weed-out" approach, targeting high failure and attrition rates to let only the brightest and most committed through. It is a near certainty in such cases that many bright and committed women will conclude that they are not bright or committed enough and select themselves out.

The second recommendation is to accommodate a wide range of computing experience among incoming students. Doing so will not only enhance recruiting of women; it will also help to recruit students from a variety of disadvantaged populations, as well as many highly talented students who simply did not become interested in computing until later in their lives. Depending on existing curricular structure, this can require minor or major changes. If curricula are deep in prerequisites and tightly scheduled, they might need to be relaxed before a multipath entry to the curriculum can become possible. Once the curriculum accommodates novice students, it is then sensible to recruit and admit students based primarily on talent and promise rather than specific hacking experience.

Our third recommendation, echoing the views of many authors, is to develop an awareness in both the curriculum and the culture of the many facets and impacts of computing. This means providing students, early in their careers, with opportunities to see the technology at work in practice. It means contextualizing the work they are asked to do, so they can understand why they are being asked to do it. It means providing them with role models and career information that will help them to picture themselves as professionals in the discipline. It means working not only with students but with faculty and staff, as well, to understand that there are many ways to be a successful computer scientist.

Finally, we recommend that structures be established for women students to come together for communication and support. Many women have remarked to us that they felt less discouraged by the difficulties they faced when they found that others shared them. If a department has too few women to support a computer science group, students can be encouraged to affiliate with a group of broader scope such as the Society of Women Engineers.

Our friend and colleague Sheila Humphreys from the University of California at Berkeley has two wise observations on this subject. One is that women's groups are especially effective if they play a role in the life of their department by placing representatives on committees and participating in policy decisions that affect students. The second is that they can have a subtle effect on women's perception of "critical mass." Students who belong to women's groups often have a much stronger sense of the presence and participation of women than statistics alone would suggest.

Implementation Requirements

Two items stand out for us as critical to the successful beginning of a college or university program to bring more women into computer science and help them to thrive. The first is a champion, somebody who will take the responsibility to push on the problem until results are achieved. Theories and policies are important but useless without sustained attention to the details. A substantial portion of the faculty at large must be receptive, but it takes more than receptivity to create change. Further, the person or people with accountability for the program must be in a position of appropriate authority to cause needed changes to be made.

The second point is that reform efforts must be suited to the local environment. One size does not fit all; the problem that pinches most at one institution may be a second- or third-order issue at another. Before picking a favorite intervention from the literature, from imagination, or even from our own list of recommendations, departments would be well advised to take the time to survey the local landscape, talk to students and faculty (perhaps through a nonthreatening third party), and prioritize interventions that focus on the most urgent local issues.

Epilogue: Changing the Conversation in Computer Science

Only forty years ago, women were nearly absent from medical classrooms. Our society has since learned that women are interested in medicine, excel as doctors, and bring with them sensibilities and concerns that were needed in the field but were rare before women entered the ranks of physicians (Walsh, 1977). Many women today breathe a sigh of relief and can't imagine living without women doctors. Will a similar transformation happen in computer science? Feminist theorist Carol Gilligan foresees women's participation this way: "To bring women in is not just to rectify an inequity . . . it means to change the whole conversation" (Patterson and Hall 1998). Will women computer scientists change the conversation in computer science? What will it then sound like?

One effort to change the conversation is embodied in the Institute for Women in Technology (IWT). The IWT was founded in 1998 by Anita Borg, a computer scientist and visionary advocate for women. Its mission is "to increase the impact of women on all aspects of technology and to increase the positive impact of technology on the lives of all the world's women" (IWT, n.d.).

The current core activity of the IWT is its Virtual Development Center (VDC), a collection of cooperating constituent Development Centers at a number of university computer science departments. The VDC's mission is to "generate projects that build technology that is inspired by and wanted by women," projects that "routinely bring broad human perspectives and involvement" to the fore. The VDC operates by bringing nontechnical women from diverse communities together with female students, faculty, and engineers from industry. Together, they brainstorm answers to questions like "What are the issues that face our families and communities?" and "What can technology do to help?" They then work together to define and prototype novel technology products addressing those needs. Project ideas so far have included family information systems, personal health monitors, personal security systems, and automated assists for air travelers.

This is more than just a different conversation with different participants. It is also formative in that it moves beyond talk into action and physical reality. This conversation and many more like it are needed to build a broader vision of computing that will more fully engage women and others as practitioners.

Our hope for this book is that it will provide the insights, stories and vocabulary for many such conversations. Our interviews reveal lifelong influences by parents, teachers, and peers that cast computing in a male mold. They explain how this leads to a narrowing of girls' and women's options, and often to the extinction of their nascent interest. They show that many women who might pursue computing careers end up alienated by a culture that was not made for them.

By casting light on these issues, we hope to provide some steps toward solutions. Thus, we describe interventions that have helped in specific instances to broaden participation in the study of computing. While they will not suit all circumstances or populations, they serve as proof by example that meaningful change is possible.

Looking ahead, we hope parents and teachers will discuss and reinvent the view of computing they convey to boys and girls. We hope they will portray to students in the broadest terms what computing is and who uses it. We hope faculty and administrators will rethink the assumptions that underlie the design of their programs and courses. We hope industry leaders will compete to enlist the talents of women, as well as men, in technology invention and design. Ultimately, we hope society will benefit from an open conversation, involving women and men of all backgrounds, on the best and highest uses of computing technology.

Appendix: Research Methodology

This appendix presents our interview protocols as well as additional details of our research design.

Longitudinal In-depth Interviews

At the heart of our data are in-depth longitudinal interviews with computer science majors. By the end of our four-year project, we had conducted over 230 interviews, equally divided between male and female students. We followed the 1995 incoming class of computer science majors throughout their entire four years, the 1996 class through three years, and the 1997 class for two years. We interviewed students multiple times during their college program. In addition to interviews, we collected information through classroom observations, surveys of entire incoming classes, informal interviews with computer science faculty and graduate students, online bulletin boards, student journals, and a focus group.

Summary of Data Gathering

Interviews
We used a set core of standard questions for the initial interview and for subsequent interviews. While there was an interview protocol to guide our interviews, we added investigatory questions as issues came to our attention during the interviews. Interviews generally ran for forty-five to sixty minutes.

Journals
During the second semester of the project, we asked all of the first-year students to participate in a journal-writing project. Students were instructed

to write whatever feelings and experiences they were having related to being a computer science student. We offered five dollars per journal entry. Eight students participated throughout the semester. We received seventy-seven journal entries. The journals amplify the interviews, allowing us to catch a glimpse of how the semester unfolded for the participants and to check the reliability of our interview findings.

Discussions with Faculty and Graduate Students
We held discussions with five women faculty (two tenured faculty, one assistant professor, and two lecturers) about our research and their experiences both as students and as faculty members. We held two group discussions with four to six women graduate students. Frequent informal discussions took place over a four-year span with the two male faculty members responsible for advising first-year students, other faculty members, and administrators of the department.

Classroom Observations
We regularly observed the first-year immigration course each week when different faculty presented their research work to the first-year students. We also observed introductory programming classes and the data structures course. We observed faculty pedagogy, classroom atmosphere, content of discussion, and speaking patterns.

Surveys of an Entire Class
All first-year students were surveyed about their computing history prior to Carnegie Mellon, their programming level, their apprehensions, and their interests. These data were analyzed along with our interview data. While our study was based overwhelmingly on qualitative research methods, the quantitative surveys of the entire class were useful indications of how closely our interpretations of students' narrative accounts aligned with quantitative data from the surveys.

Participants

The computer science student participants consisted of fifty-one female and forty-six male undergraduates. We interviewed the majority of first-year female computer science majors who entered between 1995 and

Table A.1
Total student interviews conducted

	Female	Male	Total
Computer science majors (two-thirds interviewed multiple times)	51	46	97
Noncomputer science majors	25	5	30
Total students	76	51	127
Total interviews			263

1998. Our sample of male students was randomly selected from the class rosters, with theoretical sampling done to ensure that there were male students in our sample whose prior-to-college computing experience level was comparable to the women's. Among the 51 computer science women students in our sample were 24 European Americans, 16 international students, 8 Asian Americans, and 3 African Americans. Among the 46 men were 28 European Americans, 7 international students, 6 African Americans, and 5 Hispanics.

Students were contacted by e-mail or telephone. We explained to them that the purpose of our study was to learn about students' decisions to major and their experiences in computer science so that the program could become inclusive of all students. We explained that all names would be held in confidence and that text would not be attributable to a particular student. Because of his administrative role, even Allan did not know the identities of the students. Each student who was willing to participate in our study signed a research release form.

We also interviewed students in other majors about their computing experiences and interests (see table A.1). Informal information-gathering interviews were also conducted with computer science graduate student women, computer science faculty members, high school students enrolled in computing, and high school computer science teachers.

Interview Protocols

With the students' permission, all interviews were tape recorded. Each interview was conducted in our project office by Jane or by Faye Miller, our research associate. The interview protocols were used as guides, posing questions and prompts to be asked during the interview, but the interviewer was free to ask them in any order that seemed appropriate for the conversation. The interviewer was free to explore any additional issues pertinent to our research that would arise during the interview, even if not specifically noted on the interview guide.

The interview protocol was designed to elicit specifics about students' history, experiences, and interests. The initial interview gathered information about the students' computing experience before attending Carnegie Mellon. It then gathered information about their first-year experiences. The second-year interviews continued to gather information about their experiences in the program.

Initial Interview Questions

1. Can you tell me the story about you and computers? (Prompt: when and how did you get interested?) Listen for and ask about
- When they became interested
- What interested them
- Who interested them
- Where they became interested
- Schooling experiences (elementary, middle, high school, summer programs, work)
- Their affective experience (love, one interest among many, mixed, slow to warm)

2. Family computing biography. Listen and ask about
- Who they lived with while growing up
- Parents' occupations
- Computer in the home
- What it was used for
- Who was the computer "expert" in the home
- Siblings

3. Can you tell me about your decision to major in computer science? Listen for and ask about
- Experiences that were particularly influential
- The experience most responsible for the decision to major
- Mentors
- Peers

- Parents
- Teachers
- Interests
- Aspirations
- Other

4. What were your reasons for coming to Carnegie Mellon?

5. Interest in computer science
- What interests you the *most* about CS?
- What interests you the *least* about CS?
- What are the projects you are drawn to?

6. Plans for the future: What do you want to do with a CS degree?

7. Experiences at Carnegie Mellon
- Classes: What is your favorite CS class? Why is it your favorite? What is your least favorite CS class? Why?
- Professors: Experiences good/bad with profs?
- Teaching assistants: Experiences good/bad with TAs?
- Atmosphere: How would you describe the atmosphere of the program?
- Peers and culture: If you were to describe characteristics of students in CS what would they be? Is this you? Do you fit in? Not fit in?

8. Programming
- What do you like about programming? Dislike about programming?
- Finish these sentences:
- I like programming because . . .
- I don't like programming because . . .

9. Cognitive strengths, preferences
- What do you regard as your academic strengths? Likes?
- What skills do you find necessary to be successful in CS? Do you have them?

10. Learning styles: What helps you learn material the best? (Listen for and ask about type of classes and teaching, such as learning by example or (trial and error.)

11. What is computer science?
- If you were going to describe computer science, what would you say?
- Describe what you like and dislike about computer science.

12. Qualities of good computer scientists: What are the qualities that make a good computer scientist?

13. Being a woman in the program
- Ask women:

    How are you experiencing being a woman in the program?

    Do any incidents come to mind that are related to being a woman in the program?
- Ask women and men:

    Ideas of why so few women in field?

    Ideas on what would have to be different to attract/excite more women?

14. Time spent on computer

15. Extracurricular activities

Sophomore and Junior Interview Guide

1. So how are things going?
- Last year: CS courses? Grades?
- This semester: CS courses? Grades?

2. What do you attribute your success to? And difficulties to?
- Listen for interest, background, experience, intellectual strengths, teaching, peers.
- What factor is most influential?

3. Interest in CS increased or decreased?

4. I like CS because . . .

5. I don't like CS because . . .

6. Programming
- Like because? Dislike because?
- What skills are necessary? Do you have them?

7. Understanding of "What is CS": How have your views changed?

8. Fit: Do you feel that you and CS are a good fit?

9. Thoughts about switching out of CS? Why? Why not?

10. Confidence: Has your confidence in your ability to do well in the major increased or decreased?

11. Learning: What helps you learn the most? Listen for
- Class size
- Contact with teachers

- Types of teaching
- Others

12. Other interests

13. What would you change about CS if you could?

14. Being a woman in CS: How are you experiencing being a woman in the program?

15. For women and men: Why do you feel that there are so few women in program?

16. Advice for new students

Senior Interview Guide

1. Ending now your four years in Carnegie Mellon computer science, what has become your major interest in computer science?

2. I like computer science because . . .
   I don't like computer science because . . .

3. What are your plans for after graduation?

4. Experiences with job market, job recruiters, finding employment

5. What is your vision of how computers can shape the future?

6. Looking back on your experience of four years in CS, what are some lasting impressions? Listen for and ask about
- What helped the most?
- What hurt the most?

7. What would your advice be to a high school senior thinking about computer science?

8. Is there anything you haven't discussed with us that you would like us to know about your experiences in computer science?

Longitudinal Data Analysis

Immediately after each interview, the interviewer wrote a narrative summary of what she noted as the salient issues. Narrative summaries, as explained by Joseph Maxwell (1996) in his book *Qualitative Research Design: An Interactive Approach*, are an attempt to keep the participants' stories as whole as possible to avoid "context stripping." We worked very hard negotiating the tension between the integrity of our data as full por-traits and the necessity of "fracturing" of the data into discrete elements so we could detect patterns across groups and categories. Analysis of each in-terview was a time-consuming and intensive process. A single interview can be filled with contradictions and "back and forthing." The research team ensured that quotes were not taken out of context and that a single interview was considered in light of the additional interviews.

The interviews and narrative summaries were discussed on an ongoing basis by our research team. Themes for coding interviews were developed on the basis of what students discussed as well as our prior knowledge and theoretical "hunches." While we began the research with preliminary hunches about which issues would be important (such as precollege com-puting experience, confidence issues, and cultural norms), many of the themes were "in vivo codes" that came from the students themselves (such as "dreaming in code," "being at the computer 24/7," "you only got in be-cause you are a girl," computing as an "acquired taste"). Each interview was coded for issues that relate to attachment to and detachment from computer science. To determine the relative weight of the different influ-ences, we had to work with frequency and intensity of the events, not just the existence of a code. The interviews were transcribed, and the tran-scripts were entered into NUD*IST, a computer program developed to as-sist in the qualitative data analysis (Gahan and Hannibal 1998).

We were aware of the risk of compromised data analysis, and we con-tinually asked ourselves how we could get the most accurate and detailed picture of the situation. Thanks to our funders, we were able to stay in one place long enough to be able to identify real and recurring trends and to ac-tually near a "saturation point." Too often research is done as a single snapshot, with much of the important dynamism left out of the image.

The student's comments below help illustrate the value of a longitudinal approach. In this one excerpt, the student makes a psychological U-turn halfway through her story. The first part describes her discomfort with feeling so far behind and so stupid in computer science. The second part describes her satisfaction with what she has learned in so little time and her recognition that one can learn a little but sound like one knows a lot. This type of "back and forthing" continued from interview to interview. Had we interviewed this student in the very beginning of her stay at Carnegie Mellon and not followed up with her, we might have assumed that she would leave the program. If we had to predict her future after this interview, we might assume that her recent positive experiences would tip the scale toward persistence:

It's just that computers are something that you can get left behind in so fast. For me, left behind is not a fun feeling. If I hadn't felt that you can catch up, you just work a little harder than they are, I probably would have dropped it because I hate feeling out of it. You might be only one week behind them, but it sounds like you are lifetimes behind them. . . . If you sound stupid in computers, you really sound stupid. I'm learning very fast. I wrote my friends, you don't come to CS a computer geek, but they don't let you leave without turning you into one. If you don't know how to do this, that, and the other thing, they make you look so stupid. . . . In one month I have learned more than I have learned in my lifetime. I have had so many students ask me, "Do you know how to write a plan file?" So when I learn it now, I sound all smart. When other people come in and don't know, I sound like I am a computer genius, and I'm like, "I only learned it a few days ago. It's not that big of a deal."

Analyzing each interview as a whole and following students over time gave us a richer account of their experiences and gave us the opportunity to analyze both the influential factors and the timing of events.

Sources and Further Reading

Introduction: Women out of the Loop

Sources

Behar, R. (1993). *Translated woman: Crossing the border with Esperanza's story.* Boston: Beacon.

Bryant, R., and Irwin, M. (2001). Taulbee survey. *Computing Research News* (March).

Camp, T. (1997). The incredible shrinking pipeline. *Communications of the Association of Computing Machinery* 40 (10) (October): 103–110.

Irwin, M., and Friedman, F. (1998–1999). Taulbee survey. *Computing Research News* (March).

Luttrell, W. (1997). *School-smart and mother-wise: Working-class women's identity and schooling.* New York: Routledge Press.

Margolis, J. (1992). Psychology of gender and academic discourse. *On Teaching and Learning* (vol. 4). Cambridge, MA: Harvard University Bok Center for Teaching.

Report of the Carnegie Mellon Symposium on Minorities in Computing. (1999). Pittsburgh: Carnegie Mellon University.

Seymour, E., and Hewitt, N. (1997). *Talking about leaving: Why undergraduates leave the sciences.* Boulder: Westview Press.

Whitney, D., Jr. (1970). *I'm glad I'm a boy! I'm glad I'm a girl!* New York: Simon and Schuster.

Further Reading

Bolt, D., and Crawford, R. (2000). *Digital divide: Computers and our children's future.* New York: TV Books.

Digital Divide Network. <http://www.digitaldividenetwork.org>.

Oakes, J. (1990). *Multiplying inequalities: The effects of race, social class, and tracking on opportunities to learn mathematics and science.* Santa Monica, CA: RAND Corporation.

Oakes, J., et. al. (2000). Diversity and coursetaking: Equity concerns in mathematics and science achievement. Paper prepared for the National Institute for Science (NISE) Forum on Diversity and Equity Issues in Mathematics and Science Education: Recommendations for a Research Agenda. Detroit, MI, May.

Signs: Journal of Women in Culture and Society 16 (1) (1990). Special issue on gender and technology.

Walton, A. (1999). "Technology versus African-Americans." *The Atlantic Monthly* 283 (1):14–18.

Wilhelm, A. (1998). Closing the digital divide: Enhancing Hispanic participation in the information age. Tomas Rivera Policy Institute. <http://www.cgs.edu/inst/trc.html>.

Chapter 1

Sources

Alper, J. (1993). The pipeline is leaking women all the way. *Science* 260: 409–411.

American Association of University Women (AAUW). (1992). *How schools short-change girls.* Washington, DC: AAUW.

Berenbaum, S. A., and Hines, M. (1992). Early androgens are related to childhood sex-typed toy preferences. *Psychological Science,* 3: 203–206.

Condry, J., and Condry, S. (1976). Sex differences: A study of the eye of the beholder. *Child Development* 47: 812–819.

Eaton, W. O. and Enns, L. R. (1986). Sex differences in human motor activity level. *Psychological Bulletin,* 100: 19–28.

Ehrlich, P. (2000). Tangled skeins of nature and nurture. *The Chronicle Review,* Sept. 22, pp. B7–B11.

Giacquinta, J. B., Bauer, J. & Levin, J. (1993). *Beyond technology's promise: An examination of children's educational computing at home.* New York: Cambridge University Press.

Goldstein, J.H. (1994). *Toys, play, and child development.* Cambridge: Cambridge University Press.

Kagan, J. (1964). The child's sex role classification of school objects. *Child Development* 35: 1051–1056.

Kimura, D. (2000). *Sex and cognition.* Cambridge, MA: MIT Press.

Maccoby, E., and Jacklin, C. (1987). *Psychology of sex differences.* Palo Alto: Stanford University Press.

Meyer-Bahnburg, H. F., Feldman, J. F., Cohen, P., and Ehrhardt, A. A. (1988). Perinatal factors in the development of gender-related play behavior: Sex hormones versus pregnancy complications. *Psychiatry* 51: 260–271.

National Telecommunications and Information Administration. (1997). *Falling through the Net.* Washington, DC: Government Printing Office.

National Telecommunications and Information Administration. (2000). *Falling through the Net: Toward Digital Inclusion.* Washington, DC: Government Printing Office.

Newson, J., and Newson, E. 1968. *Four years old in an urban community.* Chicago: Aldine.

Paley, V. G. (1984). *Boys and girls: Superheroes in the doll corner.* Chicago: University of Chicago Press.

Rheingold, H., and Cook, K. V. (1975). The contents of boys' and girls' rooms as an index of parents' behavior. *Child Development* 46: 459–463.

Schofield, J. (1995). *Computers and classroom culture.* Cambridge: Cambridge University Press.

Turkle, S. (1984). *The second self: Computers and the human spirit.* New York: Simon and Schuster.

Further Reading

Furger, R. (1998). *Does Jane compute? Preserving our daughters' place in the cyber revolution.* New York: Warner Books.

Stern, M., and Karracker, K. H. (1989). Sex stereotyping of infants: A review of gender labeling studies. *Sex Roles* 20: 501–522.

Thorne, B. (1993). *Gender play: Girls and boys in school.* New Brunswick, NJ: Rutgers University Press.

Turkle, S. (1997). *Life on the screen.* New York: Touchstone Press.

Chapter 2

Sources

American Association of University Women (AAUW). (1992). *How schools shortchange girls.* Washington, DC: AAUW.

American Association of University Women (AAUW). (1998). *Gender gaps: Where schools still fail our children.* Washington, DC: AAUW.

American Association of University Women (AAUW). (2000). *Tech-savvy: Educating girls in the new computer age.* Washington, DC: AAUW.

Anderson, R., and Ronnkvist, M. (1999). The presence of computers in American schools. In *Teachers, Learning and Computing: 1998 National Survey.* University of California at Irvine, Center for Research on Information Technology and Organizations. <www.crito.uci.edu/TLC/findings/>.

Brown, L. (1999). *Raising our voices: The politics of girls' anger.* Cambridge, MA: Harvard University Press.

Brown, L., and Gilligan, C. (1992). *Meeting at the crossroads: Women's psychology and girls' development.* Cambridge, MA: Harvard University Press.

California Basic Educational Data System. (1999–2000). <http://data1.cde.gov/dataquest/dataquest.asp>.

Cassell, J., and Jenkins, H., eds., *From Barbie to Mortal Kombat: Gender and computer games.* Cambridge, MA: MIT Press.

Chodorow, N. (1999). *The reproduction of mothering.* Berkeley: UC Press reprint.

College Board. (1999). *Advanced placement program California and national summary reports.* New York: The College Board.

Debold, E. (1997). Equity in technology: Creating media that appeals to both boys and girls. Paper presented to Microsoft, Seattle, Washington.

Eccles, J. (1989). Bringing young women into math and science. In M. Crawford and M. Gentry, eds., *Gender and thought: Psychological perspectives.* New York: Springer-Verlag.

Eccles, J. (1994). Understanding women's educational and occupational choices. *Psychology of Women Quarterly* 18: 585–609.

Educational Testing Service. (1997). *Computers and classrooms: The status of technology in U.S. schools.* Princeton, NJ: ETS.

Fennema, E. (2000). Gender and mathematics: What is known and what do I wish was known. Paper prepared for the Fifth Annual Forum of the National Institute for Science Education, May 22–23. <www.wcer.wisc.edu/nise/News Activities/ Forums/>.

Gilligan, C. (1982). *In a different voice: Psychological theory and women's development.* Cambridge, MA: Harvard University Press.

Hyde, J. S., Fennema, E., Ryan, M., and Frost, L. A. (1990). Gender differences in mathematics attitude and affect: A meta-analysis. *Psychology of Women Quarterly* 14: 299–324.

International Society for Technology in Education. (1999). Will *new teachers be prepared to teach in the digital age? National Survey on Information Technology in Teacher Education.* Santa Monica, CA: Milken Exchange on Education Technology.

Jenkins, H. (1998). Complete freedom of movement: Video games as gendered play spaces. In J. Cassell and H. Jenkins, eds., *From Barbie to Mortal Kombat: Gender and computer games.* Cambridge, MA: MIT Press.

Kafai, Y. B. (1998). Video game designs by girls and boys: Variability and consistency of gender differences. In J. Cassell and H. Jenkins, eds., *From Barbie to Mortal Kombat: Gender and computer games.* Cambridge, MA: MIT Press.

Kaiser Family Foundation. (1999). *Kids and the media @ the new millennium: A comprehensive national analysis of children's media use.* Menlo Park, CA: Kaiser Family Foundation.

Koch, Corina. (1995). Is computer time fair for girls? A computer culture in a grade 7/8 classroom. Unpublished paper, Queen's University, Kingston, Ontario.

Laurel, B. (1998). An interview with Brenda Laurel. In J. Cassell and H. Jenkins, eds., *From Barbie to Mortal Kombat: Gender and computer games.* Cambridge, MA: MIT Press.

Lehmann-Haupt, R. (1997). Girls school seeks to overcome tech gender gap. *Wired News.* <http://wired.com/news/culture/0,1284,7987,00.html>.

McDonnell, K. (1994). *Kid culture: Children & adults & popular culture.* Toronto: Second Story Press.

Schofield, J. (1995). *Computers and classroom culture.* Cambridge: Cambridge University Press.

Turkle, S. (1984). *The second self: Computers and the human spirit.* New York: Simon and Schuster.

Turkle, S. (1986). Computational reticence. In Chris Kramarae, ed., *Technology and women's voices: Keeping in touch.* New York: Pergamon Press.

Further Reading

Becker, H. (1999). *Internet use by teachers.* Report prepared by Henry Jay Becker, University of California at Irvine. <http://www.crito.uci.edu/TLC/findings/Internet-Use/startpage.htm>.

Campbell, P. (1999). Bringing girls into SMET in 1999: The state of the art. Paper presented to the annual meeting of the principal investigators of the National Science Foundation's Program for Gender Equity, Washington, DC, October 4.

Cuban, L. (2000). So much high-tech money invested, so little use and change in practice: How come? Paper presented for the Council of Chief State School Officers' Annual Technology Leadership Conference. Washington, DC, January.

Education Week. *Technology counts '98: Building the digital curriculum.* Washington, DC: Editorial Projects in Education.

Electronic Games for Education in Math and Science. <www.taz.cs.ubc.ca/egems/home.html>.

Fausto-Sterling, A. (1985). *Myths of gender: Biological theories about women and men.* New York: Basic Books.

Greenfield, P. M. (1996). Video games as cultural artifacts. In P. M. Greenfield and R. R. Cocking, eds., *Interacting with video.* Norwood, NJ: Ablex.

Kafai, Y. (1995). *Minds in play: Computer game design as a context for children's learning.* Hillside, NJ: Lawrence Erlbaum Associates.

Sax, L. J. (1994). Mathematical self-concept: How college reinforces the gender gap. *Research in Higher Education* 35: 141–166.

Chapter 3

Sources

American Association of University Women (AAUW). (2000). *Tech-savvy: Educating girls in the new computer age.* Washington, DC: AAUW.

Brunner, C. (1997). Opening technology to girls. *Electronic Learning* 16 (4): 55.

Eccles, J. (1994). Understanding women's educational and occupational choices. *Psychology of Women Quarterly* (18): 585–609.

Grundy, F. (1998). Mathematics in computing: A help or hindrance for women? <http://www.keele.ac.uk/depts/cs/Staff/Homes/Frances/homepage.html>.

Honey, M., Moeller, B., Brunner, C., Bennett, D., Clements, P., and Hawkins, J. (1991). Girls and design: Exploring the question of technological imagination. New York: Banks Street Center for Children and Technology Tech. Report No. 17.

IBM advertisement. (2000). *Ed Week,* June 21, p. 13.

Kramer, P., and Lehman, S. (1990). Mismeasuring women: A critique of research on computer ability and avoidance. *Signs: Journal of Women in Culture and Society* 16 (1): 158–172.

Linn, M. D., and Hyde, J. S. (1989). Gender, mathematics, and science. *Educational Researcher* 18 (8): 17–27.

Martin, D. (1992). In search of gender-free paradigms for computer science education. In C. Martin and E. Murchie-Beyma, eds., *In search of gender-free paradigms for computer science education.* Eugene, OR: ISTE.

Miller, J. B. (1976). *Toward a new psychology of women.* Boston: Beacon Press.

Rosser, S. (1990). *Female-friendly science: Applying women's studies methods and theories to attract students.* New York: Pergamon Press.

Schofield, J. (1995). *Computers and classroom culture.* Cambridge: Cambridge University Press.

Further Reading

Gilligan, C. (1982). *In a different voice.* Cambridge, MA: Harvard University Press.

Honey, M. (1994). The maternal voice in the technological universe. In D. Bassin, M. Honey, and M. Kaplan, eds., *Representations of motherhood* (pp. 220–239). New Haven: Yale University Press.

Margolis, J., Fisher, A., and Miller, F. (2000). Caring about connections: Gender and computing. *Technology and Society* 18 (4) (Winter): 13–20.

Chapter 4

Sources

American Association of University Women (AAUW). (2000). *Tech-savvy: Educating girls in the new computer age.* Washington, DC: AAUW.

Eccles, J. (1994). Understanding women's educational and occupational choices: Applying the Eccles et. al model of achievement-related choices. *Psychology of Women Quarterly* 18: 585–609.

Elkjaer, B. (1992). Girls and information technology in Denmark: An account of a socially constructed problem. *Gender and Education* 4: 25–40.

Hapnes, T., and Rasmussen, B. (1991). The production of male power in computer science. In I. V. Eriksson et al., eds., *Women, work, and computerization.* Amsterdam: North-Holland.

Kakutani, M. (2000). When the geeks get snide: Computer slang scoffs at wetware (the humans). *New York Times,* June 27, p. B1.

Levy, S. (1984). *Hackers: Heroes of the computer revolution.* London: Penguin.

Raymond, E. S. (1996). *The new hackers' dictionary* (3rd ed.). Cambridge, MA: MIT Press.

Spertus, E. (1993). *Why are there so few female computer scientists?* AI Technical Report 1315, Massachusetts Institute of Technology, Artificial Intelligence Lab.

Further Reading

Cherney, L., and Weise, R., eds. (1996). *Wired women.* Seattle: Seal Press.

Hafner, K., and Lyon, M. (1996). *Where wizards stay up late: The origins of the internet.* New York: Simon & Schuster.

Kiesler, S., Sproull, L., and Eccles, J. (1985). Pool halls, chips, and war games: Women in the culture of computing. *Psychology of Women Quarterly* 9: 451–462.

Sproull, L., Kiesler, S., and Zubrow, D. (1987). Encountering an alien culture. In S. Kiesler and L. Sproull, eds., *Computing and change on campus* (pp. 173–195). New York: Cambridge University Press.

Ullman, E. (1997). *Close to the machine: Technophilia and its discontents.* San Francisco: City Lights Books.

Chapter 5

Sources

Brainard, S., and Carlin, L. (1997). *A longitudinal study of undergraduate women in engineering and science.* ASEE/IEEE Frontiers in Education Conference, Pittsburgh.

Fiorentine, R. (1988). Sex differences in success expectancies and causal attributions: Is this why fewer women become physicians? *Social Psychology Quarterly* 51: 236–249.

Fuller, H., et. al. (1997). Attitude about engineering survey, Fall 1995 and 1996: A study of confidence by gender. In *Proceedings of the American Society for Engineering Education Annual Conference,* Milwaukee.

Sax, L J. (1994). Mathematical self-concept: How college reinforces the gender gap. *Research in Higher Education* 35: 141–166.

Seymour, E., and Hewitt, N. (1997). *Talking about leaving: Why undergraduates leave the sciences.* Boulder: Westview Press.

Spertus, E. (1991). Why are there so few female computer scientists? AI Technical Report 1315. Massachusetts Institute of Technology, Artificial Intelligence Lab.

Sproull, L., Kiesler, S., and Zubrow, D. (1987). Encountering an alien culture. In S. Kiesler and L. Sproull, eds., *Computing and change on campus* (pp. 173–195). New York: Cambridge University Press.

Steele, C. (1992). Race and the schooling of black Americans. *Atlantic Monthly* (April): 68–78.

Steele, C. (1997). A threat in the air: How stereotypes shape intellectual identity and performance. *American Psychologist* 52 (6): 613–629.

Valian, V. (1998). *Why so slow? The advancement of women.* Cambridge, MA: MIT Press.

Zeldin, A., and Pajares, F. (2000). Against the odds: Self-efficacy beliefs of women in mathematical, scientific, and technological careers. *American Educational Research Journal* 37 (1): 215–246.

Further Reading

Arnold, K. D. (1992). The Illinois valedictorian project: Academically talented women ten years after high school graduation. Paper presented at the annual meeting of the American Educational Research Association, San Francisco, April.

Astin, A. W. (1993). *What matters in college? "Four critical years" revisited.* San Francisco: Jossey-Bass.

Davis, C., et. al. (1996). *The equity equation: Fostering the advancement of women in the sciences, mathematics, and engineering.* San Francisco: Jossey-Bass.

Kiesler, S., Sproull, L., and Eccles, J. (1985). Pool halls, chips, and war games: Women in the culture of computing. *Psychology of Women Quarterly* 9: 451–462.

Steele, C., et al. (1993). Self-image resilience and dissonance: The role of affirmational resources. *Journal of Personality and Social Psychology* 64 (6): 885–896.

Chapter 6

Sources

Dweck, C. (1986). Motivational processes affecting learning. *American Psychologist* (October): 1040–1048.

Garland, M. (1993). The mathematics workshop model: An interview with Uri Treisman. *Journal of Developmental Education* 16 (3): 14–22.

Leggett, E. (1985). Children's entity and incremental theories of intelligence: Relationships to achievement behavior. Paper presented at the meeting of the Eastern Psychological Association, Boston (March).

Rayman, P., and Brett, B. (1993). *Pathways for women in the sciences. The Wellesley report. Part I.* Wellesley, MA: Wellesley College Center for the Study of Women.

Seymour, E., and Hewitt, N. (1997). *Talking about leaving: Why undergraduates leave the sciences.* Boulder: Westview Press.

Stevenson, H., and Stigler, J. (1992). *The learning gap: Why our schools are failing and what we can learn from Japanese and Chinese education.* New York: Touchstone.

Suzuki, S. (1978). *Violin school.* New York: Warner Books.

Treisman, U. (1992). Studying students studying calculus: A look at the lives of minority mathematics students in college. *The College Mathematics Journal* 23 (5): 362–372.

Further Reading

Barinaga, M. (1994). Women in science '94: Comparisons across cultures. *Science* 263: 1467–1496.

de Verthelyi, R. F. (1997). International female graduate students in engineering at a U.S. university: Survival of the fittest? *Journal of Women and Minorities in Science and Engineering* 3 (4). New York: 245–264.

Chapter 7

Sources

Failing at Fairness, Part I. (1992). *NBC Dateline.* Broadcast April 7, 1992. Burlington, VT: New Video.

National Science Foundation. (1999). *Women, minorities, and persons with disabilities in science and engineering, 1998.* Washington, DC: Government Printing Office.

Sanders, J. (1994). *Lifting the barriers: 600 strategies that really work to increase girls' participation in science, mathematics, and computers.* New York: Jo Sanders.

Sanders, J. (1995). Girls and technology: Villains wanted. In S. Rosser, ed., *Teaching the majority: Breaking the gender barrier in science, mathematics, and engineering* (pp. 147–159). New York: Teachers College Press.

Sanders, J., and McGinnis, M. (1991). *Counting on computer equity: A quick and Easy guide for finding out if your school has a computer gender gap.* New York: Scarecrow Press, Women's Action Alliance.

Further Reading

Chiang, C., Kafai, Y., and Marshall, S. (2000). Spaces for change: Gender and technology access in collaborative software design. *Journal of Science Education and Technology* 9 (1): 45–56.

Dweck, C. (1986). Motivational processes affecting learning. *American Psychologist* (October): 1040–1048.

Furger, R. (1998). *Does Jane compute? Preserving our daughters' place in the cyber revolution.* New York: Warner Books.

Gurer, D. (1995). Pioneering women in computer science. *Communications of the ACM* 38 (1): 45–54.

Sadker, M., and Sadker, D. (1994). *Failing at fairness: How America's schools cheat girls.* New York: Scribner's.

Sanders, J. (1999). Attribution, learned helplessness, self-esteem, and achievement. Paper presented to the Carnegie Mellon Summer Institute for Advanced Placement Computer Science Teachers, Pittsburgh.

Weiner, B. (1974). *Achievement motivation and attribution theory.* Morristown, NJ: General Learning Press.

Chapter 8

Sources

Rosser, S. (1990). *Female-friendly science: Applying women's studies methods and theories to attract students.* New York: Pergamon Press.

Further Reading

Blum, L. (2001). Women in computer science: The Carnegie Mellon experience. <http://www.cs.cmu.edu/~women/>, accessed February 1, 2001.

Hammond, R. (2001). Computer science opens its doors to women. *Carnegie Mellon Magazine* 19 (3): 12–17.

Epilogue

Sources

Institute for Women in Technology Mission Statement, n.d., <http://www.iwt.org/whyweexist.html>.

Patterson, M., and Hall, M. (1998). Interview with Carol Gilligan. *Pittsburgh Post-Gazette,* April 22, pp. D1–D3.

Walsh, M. R. (1977). *Doctors wanted, no women need apply: Sexual barriers in the medical profession, 1835–1975.* New Haven: Yale University Press.

Appendix

Sources

Gahan, C., and Hannibal, M. (1998). *Doing qualitative research using QSR NUD*IST.* Thousand Oaks, CA: Sage.

Maxwell, J. A. (1996). *Qualitative research design: An interactive approach.* Thousand Oaks, CA: Sage.

Index